other books by Ray Miller:

Vol. 1 FROM HERE TO OBSCURITY   Model T Fords
Vol. 2 HENRY'S LADY   Model A Fords
Vol. 3 THE V-8 AFFAIR   Early V-8 Fords
Vol. 4 THUNDERBIRD!   Ford's T-Bird
Vol. 5 NIFTY FIFTIES Fords   Post-War V-8 Fords
Vol. 6 MUSTANG Does It!   Ford's Mustang

Vol. 1 CHEVROLET: Coming of Age   1911-1942 Chevrolets
Vol. 2 CHEVROLET: USA #1   1946-1959 Chevrolets
Vol. 3 The Real CORVETTE   Chevrolet's Sports Car
Vol. 4 CAMARO!   Chevy's Classy Chassis

MUSTANG

Does It!

An Illustrated History

By RAY MILLER

The Evergreen Press
Oceanside, California

MUSTANG
Does It!

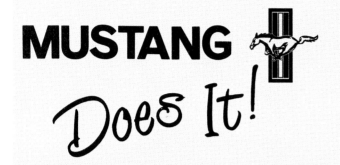

First   Printing
January   1978

Tenth   Printing
June   1982

Library of Congress Catalog Card #77-78278

ISBN 0-913056-09-X

Printed by:
  Sierra Printers, Inc.
  Bakersfield, California

Photo processing by:
  K.J.M. Photo/Graphics
  Sebastopol, California

Printed in U.S.A.

The Evergreen Press
Box 1711
Oceanside, California 92054

RAY MILLER, along with Bruce McCalley, another Founding Member of the Model T Ford Club of America, produced FROM HERE TO OBSCURITY in 1971. The book went on to become a Standard Reference for those interested in the Model T Ford, and was followed shortly by similar efforts including HENRY'S LADY, The V-8 AFFAIR, THUNDERBIRD!, and the NIFTY FIFTIES Fords. These five volumes, previously assembled as THE FORD ROAD SERIES, have been referred to as "the greatest collection of detailed information" on the Ford products, and the series is now expanded with the addition of a sixth volume, *MUSTANG Does It!*, which explores the characteristics and changes in Ford's most recent spectacular success.

Ray has been interested in cars for many years. His first, a 1933 Ford Coupe was followed by others, both Fords, and Chevrolets and his present Collection of eight cars includes representative samples from the earliest, a 1910 Model T touring car, to the latest, a 1966 Mustang GT Convertible. He drives many of his cars on a daily basis, logging thousands of miles per year in the search for outstanding and interesting automobiles.

His home, located in Oceanside, affords him the opportunity to view a wide variety of excellent examples. So many original, unrestored, and unmodified cars are still used every day here that it is a less difficult task to locate good examples in Southern California than it might be anywhere else. Visitors from the East never fail to be impressed by the exceedingly large numbers of "old" cars that may be seen daily on the freeways. With his ability to select just exactly the *right* one to illustrate the point, Ray's efforts in this direction have produced a major contribution to the recording of Automotive History.

The Author wishes to thank those who contributed so much of their time and their interest towards making this a better book than it might otherwise have been.

The Owners, generally mentioned by name within the text of this book are again thanked. Their patient understanding of the needs of this photographer, and their willingness to share with him the nuances of their own special discoveries have advanced the cause. Their patience in allowing us to crawl over, under, and through, their beautiful automobiles has permitted us to present these unique views.

Our friend, WILLIAM S. JACKSON, of Hummelstown, Pennsylvania is deserving of special mention. His willingness to assist us by photographing cars in his area added to this book, and his expertise enabled us to check several factors affecting our text.

Many other people, volunteering gladly of their specialized knowledge and experience aided us greatly. In particular, the "professionals" of this hobby, HAROLD LOONEY of Vintage Auto Parts in Orange, California, JOHN BAUM, of Special Interest Cars in Westminster, CHARLIE JONES of Obsolete Ford Parts in Nashville, Georgia, TOM TLUSTY, of Muscle Parts in Dearborn, and BILL NORTON, of Valley Obsolete Ford Parts in North Hollywood, California, all supplied helpful information and took time to verify items that we questioned.

RICK KOPEC of the Shelby-American Automobile Club enthusiastically prepared a detailed chart to guide our camera in recording subtle changes in the Shelby cars, and TOM McRAE and JOHN ZEE of Dixon Ford in Carlsbad provided, from their personal experiences and records additional information regarding the similarities and the differences between the Fords and Shelbys.

GRANT MERRILL, of Poway, California, a friendly and outgoing enthusiast guided to our camera several cars that we might otherwise not have seen including the rare T-5 model found on page 121. JIM PETRIK, of Madeira, Ohio, supplied catalogs on this and on the earliest models.

LARRY WEIS of the Public Relations Department of Ford Motor Company was able to provide considerable background information as well as a tabulation of the production figures found herein.

To all of these, and to the far greater number whose names do *not* appear, we again express our gratitude for their interest, their help, and their encouragement. This book is a better effort for their help.

rjm

In 1964, one Automobile Manufacturer broke through the ho-hum barriers of conservative design and produced an entirely new model intended to satisfy the interests of *several* segments of his Market. This car, with its lengthened and extended hood, fore-shortened rear deck, sculptured body panels, and sporty bucket seats succeeded in providing a family-size sedan for the super-market crowd, a "youthful abandon" appearance for those whose memories dwelt with the earlier two-passenger Thunderbird, abundant power and control options for the soon-to-be-called "macho" segment, and a platform on which the speed-oriented could bolt readily available added power and handling accessories to convert it to an all-out sports car/racing machine.

The Manufacturer was the Ford Motor Company, and the car was MUSTANG! That Ford's project was right on its target is attested to by the fact that the car found over 100,000 buyers in its first *four* months, a half million more in the next twelve, and it reached a total of well over *one million cars* in fewer than twenty-four months! Mustang's initial sales set an unequalled record that has yet to be eclipsed.

Its very success resulted in the production of similar cars (its name even provided their description: "pony cars") by other manufacturers and the competitive race was on. The result was to be a departure from the original concepts and by 1973, Mustang had grown some 12 inches in length and almost 20% in weight. No longer "the car that was designed to be designed by you", it yet remained the choice of loyalists, but offered those who preferred something "different" little reason for its selection. Thus, Ford Motor Company, in an unusual reaction, achieved another notable success when it produced the more compact 1974 model, making the first time the Industry had down-sized a successful line of its cars.

The factors that made the original MUSTANG the outstanding popular choice that it became in the mid-Sixties remain effective. Less than a dozen years later they are already inspiring Collectors to seek the more desirable models. In some circles it is already believed that the early Mustangs will soon join the ranks of the outstanding collectible automobiles of earlier years.

In the early 1960's, Ford Division was headed by a young man whose rise through the Company's ranks had been through the Sales Department. A Mechanical Engineer by education, he had joined Ford as a Trainee shortly after achieving his Master's Degree at Princeton University.

With a background of almost 15 years in the Company's various Sales Division, this man had been adequately trained to study and detect the moods of his Market, and noted an apparent need for a new, luxurious, "small" car, a product with which the Company might meet and defeat the growing Import Car market.

His solution was radical—build a basic vehicle with "pizazz", the Detroit word for Glamour, Vitality, Excitement. Reduce the wheelbase, lengthen the hood, shorten the rear deck, and lower the roofline. Then, offer endless luxury "options" to allow the buyer essentially to customize his purchase.

For his perception of the Market, his understanding of its desires, his commitment to his project, and his own ability to lead his Staff to what was to become the most successful new-car introduction of all time, this book is dedicated to the Ford Division's then-General Manager, Lee A. Iacocca.

In presenting his material, the Author has made no attempt to isolate the cars except by model year. Since we have been attempting to describe the *characteristics* of a given year, we have deliberately employed those pictures which best served the immediate purpose. *For this reason, adjacent photos may not necessarily show views of the same car.*

We have attempted to screen the inaccuracies; we trust that we have succeeded in this effort. The book was intended to be what it is, a compendium of information that will enable an observer to identify and to classify both cars and also parts. If there are errors, they are neither to our knowledge nor are they intentional.

TABLE OF CONTENTS

Introduction 15

1964½ "The Ford Mustang" 26

1965 "Total Performance Mustangs" 46

GT 350 "Shelby-American's Sports Cars" 66

GT 350H "Let Hertz put You in the Sports-Driver's Seat" 90

Mustang GT "Unique Ford GT-Striped Performance" 96

1966 "Mustang! Mustang! Mustang!" 100

T-5 "A Mustang that isn't a 'Mustang' " .121

Typical 1965/66 Accessories 122

Engines and Transmissions 132

1967 "Three new ways to answer the Call" 142

Shelby GT "The Road Cars" 182

1968 "Better Ideas in Action" 188

GT/CS "California Made It Happen" 206

Shelby GT "Drive the Race-Proved Road Cars" 210

1969 "All-New Mustangs" 218

Boss cars "Muscle Mustangs" 232

Shelby GT "Fire and Refinement" 238

1970 "Mustang's Got Personality" 246

1971 "Sparkles Like Champagne" 262

1972 "Sporty, Personal, Better Idea" 276

1973 "Mustang's last Convertible" 290

Gas Caps 302

Wheelcovers 305

Appendix 314

¹mus·tang \'mə,staŋ\ n -s [MexSp mesteño, mestengo, fr. Sp. animal without an owner, stray, fr. mesteño, mestengo, adj., ownerless, strayed, fr. mesta, annual roundup of cattle formerly held in Spain, annual meeting of the owners of such cattle that disposed of strays, fr. ML (animalia) mixta mixed animals, fr. L animalia animals + mixta, neut. pl. of mixtus, past part. of miscēre to mix — more at MIX] **1 a :** the small hardy naturalized horse of the western plains directly descended from horses brought in by the Spaniards — compare CAYUSE 3, INDIAN PONY **b :** BRONCO **2** slang **:** a commissioned officer (as in the U. S. Navy) who has risen from the ranks **3 :** SPHINX **4**
²mustang \"\ vi -ED/-ING/-s **:** to hunt wild horses

In a subsequent coincidence, the assembly facilities of Shelby-American in Los Angeles, shown here in 1965, were later to become the facility in which North American Aviation would house production of their T-39 Sabreliner jet airplane.

A decade earlier another Automobile Manufacturer, seeking an innovative and exciting new name for his about-to-be-introduced sports car, ignored the depreciating effect of the dictionary's definition, relied instead on the charisma gained during the previous War by slashing, quick, darting Navy frigates and called his new car the "Corvette".

Whether by coincidence, or by design, a choice was made by the Ford Motor Company in 1964 to give their new and exciting model the same name as that of yet another of World War Two's mechanical heroes. That Mustang was, in its way, also a clean, streamlined, well-balanced and powerful machine, and its early versions served as suitable platforms for added growth as more and more powerful engines and armaments became available.

P-51 MUSTANG FIGHTER

A veteran of two wars—World War II and the Korean War—North American Aviation's F-51 Mustang was the first United States fighter airplane to push its nose over Europe after the fall of France. Then called the P-51, it scurried back and forth across the channel, taking on the best the Axis could put in the air. Mustangs met and conquered every German ship from the early Junkers to the sleek, twin-jet Messerschmitt 262s.

Although first designed for the British as a medium-altitude fighter, the Mustang excelled in hedge-hopping strafing runs and long-range escort duty. It made a name for itself by blasting trains, ships, and enemy installations in western Europe and by devastating Axis defenses prior to allied invasion of Sicily and Italy.

An amazing array of firsts was piled up by the Mustang while carrying the war to the heart of the German fatherland. It was the first single-engined plane based in Britain to penetrate Germany, first to reach Berlin, first to go with the heavy bombers over the Ploesti oil fields and first to make a major-scale all fighter sweep specifically to hunt down the dwindling Luftwaffe.

One of the highest honors accorded to the Mustang was its rating in 1944 by the Truman Senate War Investigating Committee as "the most aerodynamically perfect pursuit plane in existence."

Added to their many marks of military distinction are two feats of Captain Charles F. Blair. In January 1951, Captain Blair set a new non-stop trans-atlantic record when he flew his flame-red Mustang from New York to London in 7 hours and 48 minutes.

On May 29, Captain Blair piloted his Mustang from Bardufoss, Norway, across the North Pole to Fairbanks, Alaska—a distance of 3450 miles—in 10 hours and 29 minutes. This is the first time that any man has made a solo flight over the pole in a single-engine airplane.

In setting his new mark, Blair, a commercial airline pilot with more than 420 Atlantic crossings and over 18,000 hours in the air, praised his F-51 as an unusually safe airplane to pilot. Not once in his history-making trans-polar flight did he feel in danger, he stated. His further comment on the Mustang is typical from seasoned pilots or from new pilots. Captain Blair said that the flight in his Mustang was "an easy one".

. . . North American Aviation Company Press Release

*I*n 1960, the "Wonderful New World of Ford" included a wide range of products. At the top of the line were two Thunderbirds, now a four-passenger well-received luxury car departing greatly from its initial two-seated "personal car" model. The "big" Ford line of Galaxie cars (enhanced by the Starliner Hardtop and the Sunliner Convertible) provided three more choices, and two Fairlane 500 mid-priced models, along with three budget Fairlanes, offered a wide selection of "conventional" cars. In addition, there were five station wagon choices ranging from the top-of-the-line Country Squire to the economy two-door Ranch Wagon.

Although this line-up provided Buyers with a selection of twenty different vehicles from which to chose, Ford now presented their new Falcon, an entirely new offering. A "New-Size" Ford, Falcon was a well-proportioned, economical, six-cylinder smaller car. With a brand-new six cylinder 90 horsepower engine, it promised "up to 30 miles per gallon . . . in typical average driving", and its advertising emphasized its front-mounted engine, available automatic transmission option, Safety Construction, and its "manufacture in Dearborn, Michigan, automotive capital of the world", all statements clearly in defiance of the then-burgeoning Import Car Market (especially that of the popular Volkswagen).

First assembled on September 14, 1959, Falcon was to be extremely well received. It provided Buyers with a *domestic* alternate to the imported car, and it was certainly true that Ford's established network of Service Departments would far exceed that of the Imports. One *million* new Falcons were built in its first 26 months, yet Falcon was never aimed at what was shortly to be identified as a large market segment. This was the up-coming "youth" Market, that large group of post-war babies who, in the mid-Sixties, would reach their age of automotive decision. What would *their* interests be, wondered Ford. Accordingly, Market Surveys were performed which indicated that the large percentage of the coming new buying group would want such "sporty" items as bucket seats, four-speed transmission, high performance engines, in short, a more "sporty" car.

*"a MUSTANG is for riding in the open!
a MUSTANG is for riding in to town!
a MUSTANG will cheer you when you're
    moping!
'specially when the top is neatly down!"*

Ford promotional jingle, Spring, 1964

* * * * * * * * * *

Basic parameters for an entirely new vehicle were established by late in 1961: the car was to be not more than 180 inches long, weigh not more than 2500 pounds, cost under $2500. Its engine was to be a standard six-cylinder with a V-8 optionally available, and above all, it was to be "demure enough for church-going, racy enough for the dragstrip, and modish enough for the country club". Such were the guidelines to which Ford's Design Staff would work.

* * * * * * * * * *

Thus was created within Ford the genesis of what was to become the world's most successful new car, and by early 1962, the name Mustang was first placed on an experimental two-seated sports car built by Ford's Engineering Department. Powered by a 91.4 cid V-4 produced by Ford of Germany, the engine was located at the rear, just forward of the axle, and was rated at 109 horsepower with a two-barrel carburetor. This first *MUSTANG* was built on a steel cage formed of one-inch tubes with appropriate sheet metal gussets and reinforcements, and its body skin was aluminum sheet, the assembly thus providing great strength at low weight.

The *MUSTANG* had a short, 90 inch wheel base, and standard front disc brakes, independent rear suspension, 13" cast magnesium wheels, built-in roll bar, and highly advanced aerodynamic styling. Its unique features included the use of two separate radiators, one on each side, placed just behind the

Built on a 90 inch wheelbase, and only 154 inches overall, the 1962 Mustang, featuring a rear-mounted engine, was an experimental two-passenger sports car. Large scoops on its sides directed air through engine coolant radiators, and a now-familiar emblem appeared on its front fenders.

Mustang II, circa 1963, featured more conventional front-mounted engine and offered a removable hardtop but was not equipped with bumpers.

highly visible external air inlet scoops. Another was the use of a fixed seat (which added to rigidity) and adjustable control pedals. The accelerator, clutch, and brake pedals were mounted on a fixture which allowed for up to four inches of fore-and-aft travel.

In all, the original *MUSTANG* was a highly innovative vehicle and provided later versions with both a name, and the now-familiar running-horse emblem found on its sides which was later used on the production vehicles. In a later re-writing of a Series designation (the Lincoln-Continental experienced a similar revision), this first approach would become known as the *"Mustang I"*, a designation it did not bear in contemporary life.

* * * * * * * * *

THE EVOLUTION OF FORD MOTOR CO. EXPERIMENTAL AND SPORTS PROTOTYPE VEHICLES

1962	MUSTANG I *EXPERIMENTAL SPORTS*
1963	MUSTANG II *EXPERIMENTAL SPORTS*
1964	MUSTANG *FORD DIVISION PRODUCTION VEHICLE* — FORD MARK I-A GT-40 *F.I.A. GT PROTOTYPE*
1965	FORD MARK I-A GT-40 *F.I.A. GT PROTOTYPE* — FORD MARK II *F.I.A. SPORTS PROTOTYPE* — FORD X-1 *EXPERIMENTAL MODIFIED SPORTS*
1966	MACH I *EXPERIMENTAL SPORTS* — FORD GT-40 *F.I.A. PRODUCTION SPORTS* — FORD MARK II-A *F.I.A. SPORTS PROTOTYPE* — FORD "J" CAR *EXPERIMENTAL SPORTS PROTOTYPE*
1967	MACH II *EXPERIMENTAL SPORTS* — FORD MARK III *LIMITED PRODUCTION STREET VEHICLE* — MIRAGE *J.W. ENGINEERING F.I.A. SPORTS PROTOTYPE* — FORD MARK II-B *F.I.A. SPORTS PROTOTYPE* — FORD MARK IV *F.I.A. SPORTS PROTOTYPE*

A widely circulated "family tree" illustrates the relationship between a number of vehicles.

During the summer of 1962, a "competition" was staged among Ford's three Design Studios (Corporate Projects, Ford Division, and Lincoln-Mercury). Given only the overall dimensions, the three groups were challenged to present their concepts in the form of clay models within only two weeks! Seven proposals were received; of them one stood out above all others and formed the basis for the production vehicle which was virtually unchanged in appearance from the clay. That version was the submission of the Ford Division's own Studio.

Later, in September of 1962, funds were authorized for the design and production of a new car with a target date for the assembly of the first production model, Job #1, to be March 9, 1964, a scant 18 months later!

* * * * * * * * *

In the Spring of 1963, the public saw Ford's *MUSTANG II* for the first time as it was driven around the track at Watkins Glen in New York. This version, now on a 108" wheelbase, some 18 inches longer than the two-passenger *MUSTANG*, was introduced as a "two-plus-two" which meant that it was designed comfortably to accommodate two front-seat passengers plus two more passengers in a minimal rear seat area. Although its removable hardtop and its attractive headlight grills did not make it into subsequent production cars, several of MUSTANG II's features did.

The Mustang II had a conventional front-mounted engine, thus abandoning the rear-mounted engine, transaxle, and independent rear springing found on the *MUSTANG I*. Further, the engine was the 289 cid 4 barrel carburetor-equipped V-8, a powerful engine that was to be offered as an option in production.

Ford's GT-40, circa 1966, an extremely effective all-out racing vehicle.

The car had "sculptured" side panels, and a mock air inlet grill trim at the sides which turns up again on the 1966 models. The short rear deck of MUSTANG II is carried forward into the production cars as is the extended hood and although the new grill is redesigned, its ornamention is familiar.

* * * * * * * * * *

Initially known as "T-5", an undistinguished code name employed in lieu of a selected name, the new project was also referred to as the "special Falcon", then the "Cougar", a name applied by the Ford Design Studio to their successful clay presentation, "Torino", reminiscent of things Italian (styling of which was then-popular), and several others. It was obvious that a "final" name must be chosen. Among those ultimately considered were several which would be discarded, but which ultimately make it to the Market on other vehicles. Included were, in addition to Torino and Cougar, the Bronco, Colt (later used by Dodge), Puma, Cheetah, and, of course, many others. Ignoring its chronological appearance as "Mustang III", the simple name was finally selected and approved.

* * * * * * * * * *

1963 was a significant year as plans progressed for the production of the new car. Market studies continued and their results were programmed back into the continuing design. Prices were studied, verified, checked, and re-checked. Decisions were made, reviewed, confirmed, and implemented, and the work continued with the target conceived as being the introduction of the new car at the opening of the World's Fair in New York City in April of 1964.

Prototypes of the new *Mustang* were shown to selected representatives of the buying public. Specifically identifiable groups such as "young marrieds" were shown the car and asked their opinions. Almost to a man over-estimating the selling price, they were initially reluctant, but later wildly enthused when informed of the "under $2500" selling price. Thus, in addition to the original "youth" market Ford found a similar enthusiasm in an older segment adding a new dimension to their advertising targets.

By early 1964, there was already a public awareness that something was brewing at Ford and on February 7, 1964, Ford confirmed to the Press that they planned to introduce a new Sport-Type car:

"The Ford Motor Company confirmed yesterday that it would introduce a new sports-type car, the Mustang, that has already been dubbed the "poor man's Thunderbird". The Mustang, a four-passenger car that will sell in the $3000 range, will have a 108 inch wheelbase, 5 inches shorter than the T-Bird, and will be about 185 inches long. A six-cylinder engine will be standard, and there will be three optional V-8 engines."

Later, in what might well have been an *intentional* promotional effort, a prototype Mustang Convertible was photographed on a downtown Detroit public parking lot. The picture was widely distributed for publication in such journals as the *New York Times* (where it appeared on March 3, 1964) and provided the public with its *first* view of the final configuration.

* * * * * * * * * *

On March 9, 1964, Job #1, the first production Mustang was assembled at the Dearborn Assembly Plant. Only 18 months had elapsed since the initial funding of the project, but an essentially new car had been designed and placed into production. Within 30 days following, over 9000 similar vehicles were produced, and by July production was commenced on a second assembly line in San Jose. Shortly thereafter the third line at Metuchen, New Jersey would also be placed into operation.

* * * * * * * * * *

Public Introduction was set for April 17, 1964, and it was a day to be remembered! Four days earlier, the Press had been invited to inspect the car in the Ford Pavilion at the New York World's Fair where top Ford executives, including Henry Ford II, displayed the new car and gained the unusual "coincidence" of placing their product on the covers of both *Time* and *Newsweek* at the same time. Other national magazines and newspapers were almost universally in agreement, most featur-

Only six weeks after its first public showing, the exciting new Mustang was selected to be the Official Pace Car at the Indianapolis Motor Speedway Memorial Day 500 mile race.

Indianapolis Motor Speedway Official Photo

17

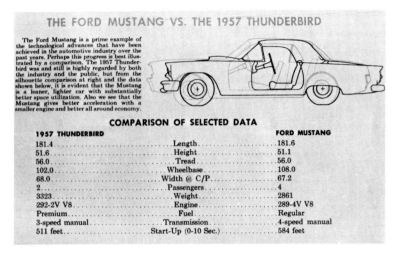

Surprisingly, Mustang has almost exactly the same overall dimensions as the 1957 two-passenger Thunderbird, yet with only a six inch longer wheelbase, it provides four passengers with a far smoother ride.

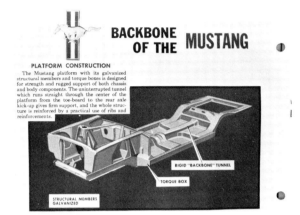

BACKBONE OF THE MUSTANG

PLATFORM CONSTRUCTION

The Mustang platform with its galvanized structural members and torque boxes is designed for strength and rugged support of both chassis and body components. The uninterrupted tunnel which runs straight through the center of the platform from the toe-board to the rear axle kick-up gives firm support, and the whole structure is reinforced by a practical use of ribs and reinforcements.

Mustang is built with "Platform Construction" which means that no sub-chassis frame is employed. After welding the body shell to this platform, an extremely rigid single integral unit is obtained.

ing complimentary and exciting editorial accounts of the car.

On the night of April 16th, Ford sponsored simultaneous commercials on all three major television Networks, and Mustang's picture was presented in the living rooms of over 29,000,000 American homes. The following day, April 17th, announcement ads appeared in over 2600 daily newspapers!

With all of these promotional efforts, the morning of April 17th found the Dealers' showrooms jammed with visitors. Along with the *expected* "incidents" came some interesting reports; over 4,000,000 people visited the showrooms that weekend; over 22,000 cars were ordered; 15 buyers competed for one car with the successful bidder refusing to leave his car for fear that it would be sold out from under him. A truck was reportedly driven into a showroom when the driver was distracted by the crowds; a car was marooned on a wash rack by a sea of visitors, a showroom was padlocked when the press of incoming crowds threatened a stampede. On and on went the reports, each of them adding to Mustang's publicity.

Other promotional projects followed; Mustangs were displayed at major Airport Terminals and at high-traffic big-city locations. Some 100 Holiday Inns gained mutual publicity when they displayed new Mustangs near their registration desks. In an unusual appeal to the woman of the family, Ford took ads in the Women's pages of almost 100 major cities' newspapers to announce that for the *first time* in its 125 year history, Tiffany had given a design award for a commercial product, the Mustang.

* * * * * * * *

The new car was an immediate hit. With its longer and lower hood and foreshortened rear deck, its "sculptured" side panels and lowered roofline, it appealed to virtually everybody. Within four months of its introduction, the Mustang had sold over 120,000 units with its attractive Hardtop Coupe outselling the more sporty Convertible by a factor of over three to one. Mustang had arrived and Mustang was here to stay!

* * * * * * * *

Introduced as a "1964½ Model", Mustang was offered at only $2368, fob Detroit. As eye-catching as *that* might have been a list of the standard items included in this figure as amazing, for they included:

Front Bucket Seats	Lighter & Ashtray
Sports Car Steering Wheel	Courtesy & Glove Box Lights
Tunnel-Mounted Shift Lever	Arm Rests
Moulded Carpets	Sun Visors
Padded Instrument Panel	Curved Window Glass
Bright Hardware	Full Wheel Covers
Suspended Accelerator Pedal	Insulated Rust-Resistant Body
Easy Action Convertible Top Latches	Bolt-On Front Fenders
16 Gallon Fuel Tank	Vinyl Headliner
Fresh Air Heater/Defroster	Counterbalanced Hood/Deck
Vinyl Upholstery	Lid Hinges
Scissors Jack	Single-Action Hood Latch
Rear-View Mirror	Twice-a-Year Maintenance
Aluminum Scuff Plate	Bright Windshield/Backlit Moulding
Extra-Wide Parallel Wipers	Color-Keyed Seat Belts
2-State Door Checks	Self-Adjusting Brakes
2 Color-Keyed Interiors	Bear-Hug Door Latches

Despite all of this, however, Mustang rarely sold for its base price for the Options were just too enticing. In concept, "the car that was designed to be designed by you", Mustang became just that, a platform on which to pile options. 50% were sold with automatic transmissions, 85% with white sidewall tires, 80% with radios, and despite Ford's admonition to its Dealers to "sell the SIX", 71% were equipped with one of the three available V-8 engines. A full 10% were sold with the "Rally-Pac", an optional tachometer/clock instrumentation pod. Options proliferated and at one point some 70 factory-offered items were available.

Initially offered only in the Hardtop Coupe and Convertible models, a new model was introduced in September. The Fastback 2+2 was presented as one of three 1965 models and offered a new concept of a two passenger car with "minimal seating" for two additional passengers in a fold-down rear seat. A popular new style, unrelated in appearance to the earlier two models, the snappy looking Fastback was to serve as a platform for what would possibly be the "ultimate option", the Shelby GT-350.

Late in 1964, Shelby-American Incorporated, in Los Angeles, builders of the race-proven AC-based Cobras would modify the first of what would later total over 13,000 "Shelby" Mustangs. With experience gained in strengthening and stiffening the earlier AC frame to accept the Ford 260 cid (and later the 289 cid) V-8 engines in place of their original 4 cylinder Bristols, Shelby had made a name in racing and was well prepared to "beef up" the basic High Performance Mustang Fastback. Over 500 were to be produced in 1965, providing a genuine off-the-shelf race car to enthusiasts, and over 2300 more appeared in 1966, most based on the 1966 Mustangs. Shelbys re-named car, the GT-350 outran their competition and in dominating the Sports Car Club of America's B Production class in 1965, 1966, and again in 1967, Shelby's car brought to the Mustang an air of authenticity genuinely deserved.

Shelby-American's "raw stock" was a Ford Mustang fastback with High Performance options which was shipped uncompleted from Ford's San Jose plant. Noticible omissions include the hood and rear seat assembly.

Dealers make promotional use of Mustang Demonstrators. Here Vince Dixon of Dixon Ford in Oceanside, California presents a new 1966 Hardtop Coupe to be used by the Welcome Wagon Hostess in furthering community relationships.

Mustang was to continue to improve its popularity in 1965, ending the year with the sale of over 550,000 units. Thus the 1966 model was little-changed and the one millionth Mustang would be produced on March 2, 1966, less than 24 months after its introduction. Following as it did a similar achievement with the Falcon on which it was based, Ford had two outstanding successes erasing some of the recollections of their disasterous experience with their Edsels.

In the early days, Mustang fathered many corollary activities and products. Clubs were formed to sponsor exciting Rallys and Road Races, and accessories were developed, many of desirable application (such as sun glasses), but some of questionable need (such as rear-bumper pony hoof bumperettes). "Mustang Mania" had struck, and virtually no one escaped the effects of the new car. Even its *name* lent itself to a whole "new breed" of small sporty cars, and "pony car" became an accepted designation.

On April 16, 1965, First Anniversary of the introduction of the Mustang, some 25,000 "Mustangers" were scheduled to compete in a "Rally Day U.S.A." program. Sponsored by the National Council of Mustang Clubs, some 250 Clubs participated in weekend rallys which included driving and various competitive events. Winners in each Rally were awarded $50 worth of Ford Accessories, and by the Company's estimate, some 12,000 Mustangs were involved.

After peaking with the production of over 600,000 units in 1966, Mustang started to slip in 1967 although over 450,000 were produced that year. Despite the introduction of the exciting and innovative Muscle Cars including the Boss 302 and the even more powerful Boss 429 (the only Mustang ever to employ the poweful 429 Hemi engine) in 1969, Mustang's popularity continued to decline. In continuing to grow in size and in weight, Mustang gained some 600 pounds and over a foot in length by 1973! The Extra-Ordinary Fine Car of 1966 was to become the Ordinary Good Car of 1973. Thus, in 1974, Ford introduced a *new* smaller Mustang II, marking the first time that an Industry Leader had down-sized a successful line of his cars.

From its antecedents in 1962 to its descendents in 1974; from the "sweetheart of the Supermarket Set" and the Desmonds and Wolfgangs of 1965, through the road-devouring Shelbys and the Muscle Mustangs of 1969-70; from the economical SIX to the fire-breathing Super Cobra Jet V-8, Mustang is all of these. In short . . .

MUSTANG *Does* It!

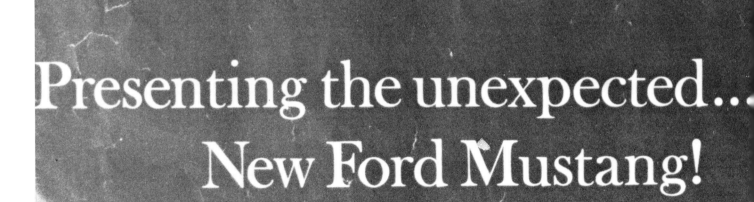

As part of a multi-million dollar advertising campaign, this advertisement appeared as part of a four-page insertion in national magazines of April 1964. It was followed by others as the months passed in what was then, and remains, the classic example of media saturation. Over ten million dollars were reported to have been spent in the initial promotion of Ford's new Mustang!

Presenting the unexpected...
New Ford Mustang!

This is the car you never expected from Detroit. It is so distinctively beautiful it has received the Tiffany Award for Excellence in American Design, the first automobile ever to be so honored by Tiffany & Co. Mustang has the look, the fire, the flavor of one of the great European road cars. Yet it is as American as its name . . . and as practical as its price. Because Mustang is an amazingly versatile car and can be inexpensively tailored to the widest variety of individual tastes, many very different people will find it surprisingly easy to say: "This is the ideal car for me." Turn the page and you'll see why.

Wolfgang used to give harpsichord recitals for a few close friends. Then he bought a Mustang. Things looked livelier for Wolfgang, surrounded by bucket seats, vinyl interior, padded dash, wall-to-wall carpeting (all standard Mustang)...and a big V-8 option that produces some of the most powerful notes this side of Beethoven. What happened? Sudden fame! Fortune! The adulation of millions! Being a Mustanger brought out the wolf in Wolfgang. What could it do for you?

Best year yet to go Ford
MUSTANG!
MUSTANG!
MUSTANG!

In one of the most fascinating advertising series ever produced, Ford presented in 1965 a succession of commercials extolling the exciting new life that awaited Mustang buyers. "Life was one diaper after another until Sarah got her new Mustang", one such ad related, but _now_, after getting her car . . .

These ads appeared not only in print, but were the basis for similar ones which appeared on television. One of the most memorable of these was one in which a conservative Henry Foster, in pince-nez glasses, dark suit, and derby is transformed into a sporty Mustang Convertible driver complete with red vest and racing goggles while voices are heard to murmur "Something's Happened to Henry!".

Life was just one diaper after another until Sarah got her new Mustang. Somehow Mustang's sensationally sophisticated looks, its standard-equipment luxuries (bucket seats, full carpeting, vinyl interior, chiffon-smooth, floor-mounted transmission) made everyday cares fade far, far into the background. Suddenly there was a new gleam in her husband's eye. (For the car? For Sarah? Both?) Now Sarah knows for sure, Mustangers have more fun.

Best year yet to go Ford
MUSTANG!
MUSTANG!
MUSTANG!

Bernard was a born loser. He couldn't win at Solitaire, even when he cheated. Enter Mustang—the car that's practical, sporty, luxurious. Your choice! Bernard chose the sporty options. Got a 289 cu. in. V-8. Four-on-the-floor. Tachometer and clock combo. Special handling package. Front disc brakes— and did Bernie's luck change! Yesterday he won San Francisco in a faro game. And now he's got his eye on New York. Mustangers always win.

Best year yet to go Ford
MUSTANG!
MUSTANG!
MUSTANG!

Desmond was afraid to let the cat out...until he got his Mustang. Mustang! A car to make weak men strong, strong men invincible. Mustang! Equipped with bucket seats, floor shift, vinyl interior, padded dash, full carpeting, more. Mustang! A challenge to your imagination with options like front disc brakes, 4-on-the-floor, big 289 cu. in. V-8, you name it. Desmond traded in his Persian kitten for an heiress named Olga. He had to. She followed him home. (It's inevitable...Mustangers have more fun.)

Best year yet to go Ford
MUSTANG!
MUSTANG!
MUSTANG!

Two weeks ago this man was a bashful schoolteacher in a small mid-western city. Add Mustang. Now he has three steady girls, is on first name terms with the best headwaiter in town, is society's darling. All the above came with his Mustang. So did bucket seats, full wheel covers, wall-to-wall carpeting, padded dash, vinyl upholstery, and more. Join the Mustangers! Enjoy a lot of *dolce vita* at a low, low price.

Best year yet to go Ford!
Test Drive Total Performance '65

FORD

MUSTANG·FALCON·FAIRLANE·FORD·THUNDERBIRD

If they're still waiting for Agnes down at the Willow Lane Whist and Discussion Group, they'll wait a long time. Agnes hasn't been herself since she got her Mustang hardtop (with its racy lines, bucket seats, smooth, optional 3-speed automatic transmission and fire-eating 200 cu. in. Six). Mustang is more car than Willow Lane has seen since the last Stutz Bearcat bit the dust. (And Agnes has a whole new set of hobbies, none of which involves cards.) Why don't you find out if there's any truth in the rumor—Mustangers have more fun?

Best year yet to go Ford

MUSTANG!
MUSTANG!
MUSTANG!

Sweetheart of
the Supermarket Set

It had to be. With non-stop thrift, with extra-nimble perform-ance, with all-around, All-American elegance, Mustang has become the sweetheart of the Supermarket Set.

They like the way it makes sense with gas. More miles per gallon is about the heart of it. They relish the way Mustang maneuvers into tight parking spots, the good performance of the 200-cubic-inch Six on the open road.

And Mustang makes people feel just great. Great at the supermarket . . . grand at the opera . . . casually elegant everywhere. (Why not, with bucket seats, snappy stick shift, plush carpeting and all the other no-cost specials that a Mustang features?)

Why not make a date for a test-drive? You, too, can go places with the sweetheart of the Supermarket Set!

MUSTANG

A PRODUCT OF *Ford*

In this famous advertisement, Mustang takes direct aim on the woman of the family and promises an ease of parking, an elegance, an economy, and room for a bundle of groceries. Not only the pride of the sporty set, Mustang had arrived in favor with what was referred to as the "Supermarket Set".

1964½

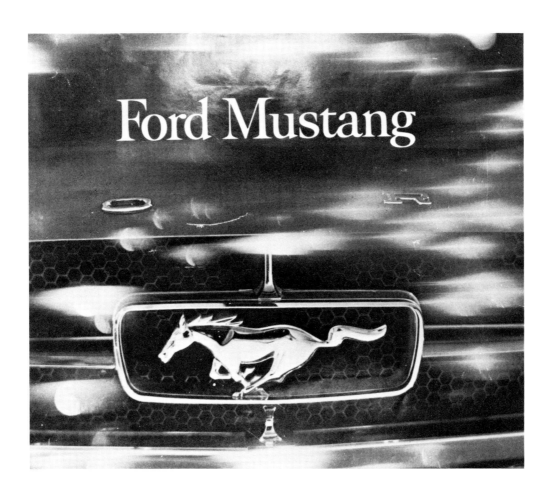

EXTERIOR COLORS

Raven Black	A
Pagoda Green	*B
Dynasty Green	D
Guardsman Blue	*F
Prarie Bronze	P
Caspian Blue	H
Rangoon Red	J
Silversmoke Gray	K
Wimbleton White	M
Sunlight Yellow	V
Cascade Green	*S
Vintage Burgundy	X
Skylight Blue	*Y
Chantilly Beige	Z
Poppy Red	3

*These colors discontinued on the 1965 models.

New Ford Mustang $2368*f.o.b. Detroit

This is the car you never expected from Detroit. Mustang is so distinctively beautiful it has received the Tiffany Award for Excellence in American Design ... the first time an automobile has been honored with the Tiffany Gold Medal.

You can own the Mustang hardtop for a suggested retail price of just $2,368—f.o.b. Detroit.

*This does not include destination charges from Detroit, options, state and local taxes and fees, if any. Whitewall tires are $33.90 extra.

Every Mustang includes these luxury features unavailable—or available only at extra cost—in most other cars: bucket seats; wall-to-wall carpeting; all-vinyl upholstery; padded instrument panel; and full wheel covers. Also standard: floor shift; courtesy lights; sports steering wheel; front arm rests; a 170 cu. in. Six, and much more.

That's the Mustang hardtop. With its four-passenger roominess and surprisingly spacious trunk, it will be an ideal car for many families. Yet Mustang is designed to be designed by you. For instance, the trip to the supermarket can be a lot more fun when you add convenience options like power brakes or steering, Cruise-O-Matic transmission, push-button radio, 260 cu. in. V-8.

Or, you can design Mustang to suit your special taste for elegance with such luxury refinements as: air conditioning; vinyl-covered roof; full-length console; accent paint-stripe; and convertible with power top.

If you're looking for action, Mustang's the place to find it, with a 289 cu. in. V-8; 4-speed fully synchronized transmission; Rally-Pac (tachometer and clock) and other exciting options.

For an authentic scale model of the new Ford Mustang, send $1.00 to Mustang Offer, Department A-1, P.O. Box 35, Troy, Michigan. (Offer ends July 31, 1964).

TRY TOTAL PERFORMANCE FOR A CHANGE!

FORD
Mustang · Falcon · Fairlane · Ford · Thunderbird

Early advertisements for the new Mustang, such as this one which appeared in May of 1964 stressed elegance reminiscent of the early Thunderbird advertising, but the bold presentation of the low $2368 selling price left little doubt that it differed.

The 1964½ Mustang was to prove to be a winner! With its exciting new appearance, its shortened rear deck and lengthened hood, it promised an excitement that it did indeed provide. Sporty bucket seats, peppy engine, and easy steering brought the car, exploited as it was, to a prominence immediately.

The achievement of _producing_ a new car in only 18 months from a start in September of 1962 was remarkable although Ford did use existing components where it could. The entire running gear was derived from the Falcons, and although 13" wheels, correct for that car, were furnished as standard, V-8 engined cars were generally delivered with the larger 14" wheels on which the car seemed to have a better appearance.

Initially the optional V-8 engine included both the 260 cid and the 4-v 289 premium fuel engine, but by June a third choice was offered, the mighty 289 High Performance version with solid lifters, heavy-duty valve train and higher compression. Even this 271 horsepower behemoth failed to strain the rugged and sturdy body. The Falcon-derived tunnelled platform with its welded-on body panels provided more than enough support for the engine.

Two models were offered, the Hardtop Coupe and the Convertible, and although both were well received, the Coupe outsold the latter by over three-to-one as more and more families accepted the closed car as both a "second car" and as their primary transporation.

All of these early models bore a "5-series" designation on their data plates, an indication that they were considered, at least statistically, as 1965 models, but those offered from April to early September are now generally referred to as "1964½" models, the name by which they were originally promoted by Ford.

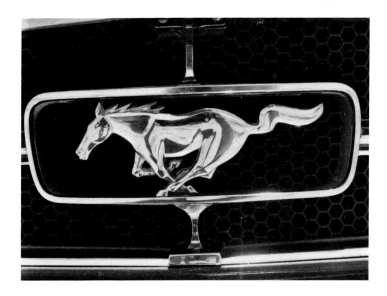

Model 65A Hardtop Coupe
Model 76A Convertible

Mustang Specifications

COLOR AND UPHOLSTERY SELECTIONS: You have a choice of 15 Mustang colors in durable, brilliant Diamond Lustre Enamel. There are 5 all-vinyl trim choices for the Hardtop and Convertible, with an additional cloth and vinyl trim for the Hardtop. Your Ford Dealer will be happy to show you actual samples of new Mustang colors and upholsteries.

MUSTANG DESIGN FEATURES: Fully Insulated and Weather-Sealed Body; Parallel-Action Single-Speed Electric Wipers; Deep-Dish Steering Wheel; Dual Sun Visors with Retention Clips; Suspended Accelerator, Clutch and Brake Pedals; Safety-Yoke Door Latches; Center-Fill Fueling; Counterbalanced Hood and Deck Lid; Sports-Type Bumpers with Guards; Easy-Action Convertible Top Latches.

ENGINES: 101-hp Mustang Six (std.)—170 cu. in. displ.; 3.50" bore x 2.94" stroke; 8.7 to 1 comp. ratio; reg. fuel; single-barrel carb.; auto. choke; self-adj. valves with hydraulic lifters.

164-hp 260 V-8 (opt.)—260 cu. in. displ.; 3.80" bore x 2.87" stroke; 8.8 to 1 comp. ratio; reg. fuel; 2-barrel carb.; auto. choke; self-adj. valves with hydraulic lifters.

210-hp 289 V-8 (opt.)—289 cu. in. displ.; 4.00" bore x 2.87" stroke; 9.0 to 1 comp. ratio; 4-barrel carb.; reg. fuel. Other specifications same as 260 V-8 above.

271-hp 4V/289 High Performance V-8 (opt.)*—289 cu. in. displ.; 10.5 to 1 comp. ratio; super prem. fuel; 4-barrel carb.; manual choke; manually adj. valves; dual exhaust.

ENGINE FEATURES: 6000-mile (or 6-month) full-flow disposable-type oil filter; 36,000-mile (or 3-year) disposable-type fuel filter and replaceable dry element air cleaner; 190° thermostat; 12-volt electrical system with 25-amp. (Six) or 30-amp. (V-8's) generator, 54-plate battery—40 amp-hr (Six), 55 amp-hr (V-8's)—and weatherproof ignition; fully aluminized muffler and tailpipe; crankcase emission control. All engines are electronically mass-balanced for long-lived smoothness.

MANUAL TRANSMISSION: 3-Speed Manual (std. with Six). Floor-mounted shift lever, standard "H" pattern. Synchronizers in 2nd and direct. **Synchro-Smooth Drive** (std. with 260 V-8). Synchronized manual shifting in all forward gears; clash-free downshifting to low while under way. Floor-mounted stick.

4-Speed Manual (opt. except 260 V-8). Sports-type close-ratio transmission, synchronized in all forward gears; floor-mounted stick.

CRUISE-O-MATIC DRIVE: (opt. except 271-hp V-8)—3-speed automatic with two selective drive ranges: 3-speed range starting in low for all normal driving; 2-speed range starting in intermediate for more surefooted driving on slippery surfaces. Floor-mounted T-bar selector with sequence: P-R-N-DRIVE-L.

FRONT SUSPENSION: Angle-Poised Ball-Joint type with coil springs mounted on upper arms. 36,000-mile (or 3-year) lube intervals. Strut-stabilized lower arms. Link-type, rubber-bushed ride stabilizer. Built-in anti-dive control.

REAR SUSPENSION: Longitudinal, 4-leaf springs with rubber-bushed front mounts, compression-type shackles at rear. Asymmetrical, variable-rate design with rear axle located forward of spring centers for anti-squat on take-off. Diagonally mounted shock absorbers.

REAR AXLE: Semi-floating hypoid rear axle; straddle-mounted drive pinion (V-8's). Permanently lubricated wheel bearings.

STEERING: Recirculating ball-type steering gear provides easy handling. Permanently lubricated steering linkage joints. Over-all steering ratio 27 to 1 (power steering 22 to 1). Turning diameter 38 ft.

BRAKES: Self-adjusting, self-energizing design. Composite drums, grooved for extra cooling; 9-in. (Six), 10-in. (V-8's). Total lining area: 131 sq. in. (Six), 154 sq. in. (V-8's).

TIRES: Tubeless, blackwall with Tyrex rayon cord, safety-type rims—6.50 x 13; 7.00 x 13 (V-8's and air conditioning).

DIMENSIONS AND CAPACITIES: Over-all length 181.6"; height 51.1"; width 68.2"; wheelbase 108"; treads—front 55.4" (Six), 56" (V-8), rear 56"; weight (approx.) 2562 lb. (Hardtop), 2740 lb. (Convertible); fuel 16 gal.; oil 4.5 qt. (Six), 5 qt. (V-8); cooling system (with heater) 9.5 qt. (Six), 14.5 qt. (V-8's); trunk luggage volume 8.5 cu. ft.

PRICES: Mustang includes heater-defroster and metal-to-metal black seat belts as standard equipment. However heater and/or seat belts may be deleted on car order if desired at an appropriate price reduction. All optional equipment and accessories, illustrated or referred to as options, optional or available are at extra cost. For the price of the Mustang with the equipment you desire, see your Ford Dealer.

*Available June, 1964

27

1964½

This car, Serial Number 5F08F 109483, was built in the Dearborn Assembly Plant on April 7, 1964, exactly ten days _prior_ to the first public showings on April 17th. A Convertible, it was well equipped, having accessories including console, V-8 Engine, Cruise-O-Matic, White Sidewall Tires, Power Steering, Rally Pac, Radio, Padded visors, Backup Lights, etc., bringing the fob price to $3411.54, a figure that did not hamper its being sold on April 18th!

1964½ Mustang Convertible   _Jack Cornely, Severna Park, Maryland_

This car, Serial Number 5R07U 102517, although having a far lower number than the one above, was actually built over ninety days later in Ford's San Jose (California) Assembly Plant which did not commence assembly of Mustangs until early in July. It is a basic Hard-top Coupe, having a six-cylinder engine, three-speed transmission and among its few options only a radio and white sidewall tires. A model such as this is estimated to have sold for closer to $2500 fob Dearborn.

1964½ Mustang Model 65A Hardtop

5F07F 169949
June 17, 1964

1964½ Hardtop Coupe
Jon Malte, Carlsbad, California

Mrs. Mary Doughty, Oceanside, California

1964½ Mustang Model 76A Convertible

Mr. Grant Merrill, Poway, California

The Mustang "corral" has integral brackets which are fastened at both top and bottom. The horizontal arms are secured to brackets behind the grill (below).

Bumper guards are standard and are identical with those furnished on the rear.

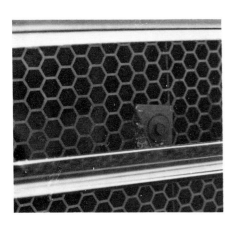

The grill features a series of octagonal cut-outs.

Adjustable rubber-tipped bumpers support the hood at either side.

A pin is used to center and latch the hood. The "handle" is secured by the secondary latches (above, left) and provides a safety catch.

The Vehicle Identification Number (VIN) is permanently stamped into the left front longitudinal strut and the fender lip is recessed to clear.

Mustang's hood opens from the front and is provided with counter-balanced hood hinges at the rear.

The wide grill is emphasized with the use of horizontal "spears" leading from the centered insignia.

The Ford name appears in individual letters, on the leading edge of the hood. The letters are castings, chromed for excellent effect.

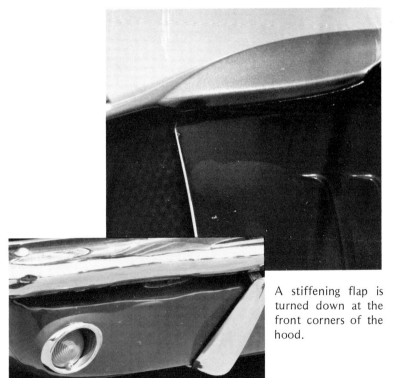

A stiffening flap is turned down at the front corners of the hood.

Parking lights with amber lenses, are installed in the lower valance panel beneath the bumpers and serve also as turn-signal indicators. Bumper guards are standard.

Simulated intake grills, decorative only, are placed astride the grill.

A wide curved windshield provides excellent visibility.

The windshield corner posts of the Convertible are trimmed in bright metal unlike those of the Coupe (right).

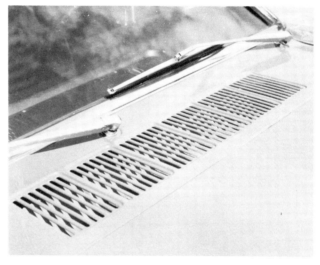

An intake air grill at the base of the windshield leads to the standard heater plenum chamber.

The standard six-cylinder engine is not commemorated (above) but the installation of one of the optional V-8 engines is marked by the use of appropriate fender insignia (photos at right). The 271 horsepower High Performance engine has an additional identification plate *behind* the 289 shield (page 136).

Deeply sculptured body side indentations are used with excellent effect.

The one-piece MUSTANG insignia is approximately 4-3/8" long (compare page 53).

The emblems on the fender are standard, but the rocker panel moulding is a dress-up option.

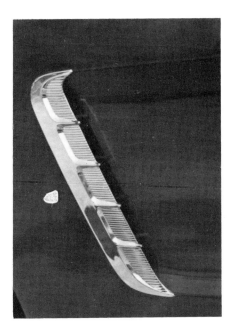

The rear quarter ornament is standard equipment, but is omitted in an "Accent Group" option which provides a side stripe and the rocker panel moulding.

The suggestion of a rear air intake is aided by the rear quarter ornament.

The door latches are described by Ford as "Bear-Hug" Safety Latches. Their scissors-like action is triggered by the fixed anchor on the door jamb.

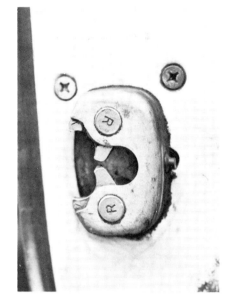

A feature of the Mustang is the use of curved side window glass. A bright-metal frame adds to its effect.

Push-button door handles are provided, and keylock is placed on both doors.

The car's data plate is riveted to the trailing edge of the left front door.

Only two-door models are built; four-door versions are not offered.

Single wide doors on each side provide easy access. The door insert is vinyl-trimmed with a heat-seamed vertical pattern.

Inside door locks are color-keyed to the interiors.

Bright all-metal window-riser and door-latch handles are secured with C-clips inserted behind their skirts. A highlight panel of contrasting pattern appears behind them.

Vent windows are latched with rotating handle and pivot manually.

Bright aluminum door sills bear the Ford insignia on a black-painted oval background.

Padded arm rests are standard and are installed on chromed plastic brackets.

1964½

The Convertible has a zippered all-vinyl rear window which can be lowered for additional ventilation. Available colors included Black, White, and Blue.

A chrome trip strip at the base of the canvas roof provides snap fasteners for the installation of a boot when top is lowered.

The area surrounding the rear window of the Hardtop is deeply embossed for heightened dramatic effect while at the same time adding stiffness to the area.

Bright metal trim frames the curved rear window of the Hardtop.

A rear package shelf is provided in the Hardtop, but none appears in the Convertible whose top folds into that area.

Standard wheels are 13", larger 14" wheels were an option. Later, after June of 1964, still larger 15" wheels were also available with the Special Handling Package.

The foreshortened rear deck of the Mustang compensated for the lengthened hood in holding the overall dimensions to 181 inches (the same as the 1957 Thunderbird), and provided a new styling feature for other manufacturers.

The rear bumper turns sharply up at its ends and protects the tail light assembly.

Back-up lights are an option but the bumperettes are standard.

The standard rear lower valance panel is not pierced for back-up lights and must be replaced (or modified) when installing that option.

The counter-balanced rear deck lid is secured by a key-operated latch.

The three "individual" lights are actually only one unit and contain a common lens. The decorative bezel adds a suggestion of individuality.

Counterbalanced hinges are provided and releasing the keylock allows lid to open easily.

Cast metal "caps" add smooth shape to rear of the fenders.

Prior to August of 1964, the Mustang Hardtop was furnished with a grey Burtex mat in the luggage compartment. Afterward, a rubber mat, as was initially used only in the Convertible, was furnished as standard. The mats are configured slightly differently on the two models.

Initially the attractive gas cap was not secured to the car. Later, possibly due to heavy thefts of this part, a wire retainer was added as a running change (see page 60).

Rear seats are cushioned to suggest comfort for two passengers, but can accommodate three.

The mounting brackets for standard sun visors differ. Coupe (above) is simpler than Convertible (right). *Padded* sunvisors were an extra-cost option.

The 1964½ steering wheel is available in five colors to match the interiors. These are Blue, Red, Ivy Gold, Black, and Parchment.

Bucket seats are standard, and the driver's seat can be adjusted fore and aft. Initially, the passenger seat was fixed, but as a running change, it too was provided with an adjusting feature.

Front seat belts are standard.

The back of the seats has a heat-sewn vertical stripe pattern.

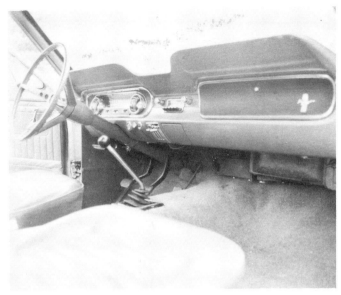

A padded cover extends protectively over the instrument panel.

A narrow trim strip secures the lower edge of the padding.

Below the steering wheel is the standard turn signal indicator lever.

At the hub of the steering wheel appears this decorative cap. However, the horn is operated by depressing one of the buttons on the spokes.

Incoming air on the driver's side is controlled by this knob below the instrument panel. Door in the heater plenum provides similar cooling for the passenger.

The parking brake is set by pulling this handle suspended at the left side below the instrument panel.

The sporty new steering wheel has what appears to be holes in its spokes. However, these are merely painted recesses.

The instrument panel of the new Mustang greatly resembles the 1964 Falcon unit from which it was derived (right).

A fuel level gauge is placed at the left.

Oil pressure and battery charting problems are indicated by illuminated OIL and GEN lights.

A temperature sensing gauge appears at the right side.

The starter is operated by the ignition key, and an optional "accessory" position is provided.

A cigarette lighter is standard equipment.

The heater is standard equipment and is controlled by this system of levers. The heater fan switch is in the "Off" position when placed at the center as shown above.

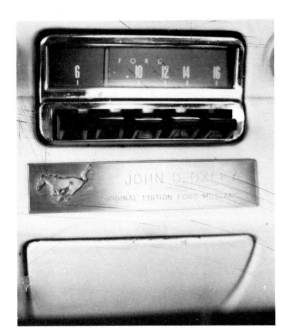

Many Dealers participated in promotional efforts by furnishing nameplates bearing the buyer's name.

The glovebox door, and instrument panel, have a grain-like metallic finish.

The Mustang emblem appears on the glovebox door.

A locking latch is offered as an accessory replacement for the standard pushbutton glovebox door latch (upper photo).

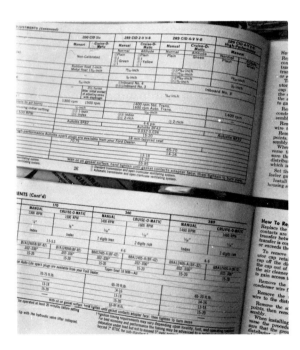

Although both are identified as Registered Owner's Manuals for the 1965 Mustang they differ. The lower copy is for the 1964½ Models and includes information on the 260 cid V-8 engine which was not offered in 1965. Other differences include the addition of the High-Performance engine Specifications (see above) and, of course, the new Fastback 2+2 description which appears in the 1965 version. Careful study of the photo at right shows transposition of panels #2 and #3.

1965

The
Total Performance
1965 MUSTANGS

		Suggested Retail
MUSTANG MODELS	**Body Code**	
2-Door Hardtop	65A	$2,320.96(2)
Convertible	76A	2,557.64(2)
2 + 2 Fastback	63A	2,533.19(2)

8-Cylinder 289 CID 2V Engine 200 HP-Extra Charge Over 200 CID 1V 120 HP 6-Cylinder	105.63

REGULAR PRODUCTION OPTIONS

ENGINES

Extra Charge Over 200 HP 289 CID 2V:	
225 HP 289 CID 4V	52.85
271 HP Hi-Performance 289 CID 4V (includes Special Handling Package and 6.95 x 14 Dual Red Band Nylon Tires – N/A with GT Equipment Group	327.92
With GT Equipment Group	276.34

TRANSMISSIONS

Cruise-O-Matic – 6-Cylinder	175.80
Cruise-O-Matic – 200 HP and 225 HP V8s	185.39
Four-Speed Manual – 6-Cylinder	113.45
Four-Speed Manual – V-8 Engines	184.02

PERFORMANCE EQUIPMENT

Disc Brakes – Front – 8-Cyl. (N/A with Power Brakes)	56.77
Limited Slip Differential	41.60
Rally-Pac – Clock/Tachometer	69.30
Special Handling Package – 200 and 225 HP V-8 Engines – includes increased Rate Front and Rear Springs, Larger Front and Rear Shock Absorbers, 22 to 1 Steering Ratio, and Larger Diameter Front Stabilizer Bar	30.64
GT Equipment Group – Available with 225 and 271 HP V-8 Engines only. Includes Dual Exhaust System with Bright Extensions through Valance Panel, Special Handling Package Components, Front Disc Brakes, Fog Lamps and Grille Bar, GT Stripe 5 Dial Instrument Cluster, and GT Ornamentation	165.03
Wheels – Styled Steel – 14" (8 Cyl. only)	119.71

POWER ASSISTS

Power Brakes	42.29
Power Steering	84.47
Power Top, Convertible	52.95

SAFETY EQUIPMENT

Emergency Flashers	19.19
Padded Visors – 65A and 76A	5.58
Seat Belts, Rear	14.78
Deluxe Seat Belts, Front – (Retractable)	7.39
DeLuxe Seat Belts, Front & Rear (Front Retractors)	25.40
Visibility Group – includes Remote Control Mirror, Day/Nite Mirror, 2-Speed Electric Wipers and Washer	35.83
Accent Group – includes body side paint stripe, rocker panel moulding – less rear quarter ornament	
65A & 76A	27.11
63A	13.90
Air Conditioner – Ford	277.20
Back up Lamps	10.47
Battery, Heavy Duty	7.44
Closed Emission System (Calif. type)	5.19
Console, full length	50.41
Console (For use with Air Conditioner)	31.52
Interior Decor Group – Includes Unique Luxury Trim, Padded Visors, Woodgrain Applique Ornamentation, and Deluxe Woodgrain Steering Wheel, 5 Dial Instrument Cluster, and R/W Door Courtesy Lights	107.08.
Full Width Seat with Center Armrest – 65A and 76A	24.42
Glass – Tinted with Banded Windshield	30.25
Windshield Only, Tinted & Banded	21.09
Radio – Push Button and Antenna	57.51
Rocker Panel Moulding – 65A & 76A	15.76
Steering Wheel, Deluxe	31.52
Vinyl Roof – 65A	74.19
Wheel Covers – Knock-Off Hubs	17.82
Wire Wheel Covers, 14"	44.83
MagicAire Heater – Delete (Credit)	(31.52)
Seat Belts – Delete (Credit)	(10.76)

1965 MUSTANG PRICES
May 15, 1965

OPTIONAL TIRE PRICES

The following Models have (5) 6.50 x 13 4-p.r. BSW Rayon Tires as Standard Equipment:

· All 6 Cylinder models

Extra charge for:	
(5) 6.50 x 13 4-p.r. WSW	33.
(5) 6.95 x 14 4-p.r. BSW	7.
(5) 6.95 x 14 4-p.r. WSW	40.

The following Models have (5) 6.95 x 14 4-p.r. BSW Tires as Standard Equipment:

· All 8 Cylinder models except with the 271 HP Hi-Performance Engine:

Extra charge for:	
(5) 6.95 x 14 4-p.r. WSW	33.
(5) 6.95 x 14 4-p.r. BSW, Nylon	15.
(5) 6.95 x 14 4-p.r. WSW, Nylon	48.
(5) 6.95 x 14 4-p.r. Dual Red Band, Nylon	48

All Models equipped with the 271 HP 289 CID 4V High Performance Engine have (5) 6.95 x 14 4-p.r. Dual Red Band Nylon Tires as Standard Equipment.

No extra charge for:	
(5) 6.95 x 14 4-p.r. BSW, Nylon	
(5) 6.95 x 14 4-p.r. WSW, Nylon	

All regular Mustang Production Options are available with the High Performance Engine except the following: Air Conditioning, 3-Speed Manual Transmission, Cruise-O-Matic, Limited Slip Differential, Power Steering, and Rayon Tires. All regular Production Options are available with the GT Equipment Group except the following: Back-up Lamps, Rocker Panel Moulding, Power Brakes, Accent Group, and Options not available with the High Performance Engine. Rear Bumper Guards are not included on GT Equipment Group Vehicles, nor is the Rocker Panel Moulding on Model 63A. Full width Seat with Center Armrest is not available with Interior Decor, GT Equipment Group, or Console Options.

46

1965 brought no major changes in Mustang; the brief period since its introduction as a 1964½ model found the demand for the car insatiable and Ford was hard-pressed to keep up with it. Three plants (Dearborn, Metuchen, and San Jose) were now building the model.

A new variant, the Fastback 2+2 was introduced on September 9th, 1964, as one of the three 1965 models, and its high performance version became the basis for conversion by Shelby-American into their exciting new GT-350.

Late in the year a new option, the "Interior Decor Group" was introduced. Featuring unique luxury trim with a Mustang-inspired seat insert, it has since become known as the "pony interior". Another interesting, but never popular, option, also a mid-year introduction, was a bench seat, available only in the Hardtop and Convertible.

Sales continued high through the year, and almost 560,000 1965 Mustangs were produced.

Mustang Specifications

COLOR AND UPHOLSTERY SELECTIONS: Pick your favorite color from 16 brilliant Diamond Lustre Enamel single tones. There are 6 all-vinyl trim choices for the Hardtop, 2+2 and Convertible, with 2 additional cloth and vinyl trims for the Hardtop and 2+2. Your Ford Dealer will be happy to show you actual samples of new Mustang colors and upholsteries.

MUSTANG DESIGN FEATURES: Fully Insulated and Weather-Sealed Body; Silent-Flo Ventilation System (2+2); Parallel-Action Single-Speed Electric Wipers; Deep-Dish Steering Wheel; Dual Sun Visors with Retention Clips (safety-padded on 2+2); Suspended Accelerator, Clutch and Brake Pedals; Safety-Yoke Door Latches; Fold-Down Rear Seat (2+2); Center-Fill Fueling; Counterbalanced Hood and Deck Lid; Sports-Type Bumpers with Guards; Easy-Action Convertible Top Latches.

ENGINES: *120-hp Six* (std.)—200 cu. in. displ.; 3.68" bore x 3.13" stroke; 9.2 to 1 comp. ratio; reg. fuel; single-barrel carb.; auto. choke; self-adj. valves with hydraulic lifters.

200-hp Challenger V-8 (opt.)—289 cu. in. displ.; 4.00" bore x 2.87" stroke; 9.3 to 1 comp. ratio; 7 main bearings; reg. fuel; 2-barrel carb.; auto. choke; self-adj. valves with hydraulic lifters.

225-hp Challenger Special V-8 (opt.)—289 cu. in. displ.; 4.00" bore x 2.87" stroke; 10.0 to 1 comp. ratio; 4-barrel carb.; prem. fuel. Other specifications same as Challenger V-8 above.

271-hp Challenger High Performance V-8 (opt.)—289 cu. in. displ.; 10.5 to 1 comp. ratio; super prem. fuel; 4-barrel carb.; manual choke; manually adj. valves; dual exhaust.

ENGINE FEATURES: 6000-mile (or 6-month) full-flow disposable-type oil filter; 36,000-mile (or 3-year) disposable-type fuel filter and replaceable dry element air cleaner; 190° thermostat; 12-volt electrical system with 38-amp. (Six) or 42-amp. (V-8's) alternator; 54-plate, 45 amp-hr battery; weatherproof ignition; fully aluminized muffler and tailpipe. All engines are electronically mass-balanced for long-lived smoothness.

MANUAL TRANSMISSION: *3-Speed Manual* (std. with Six). Floor-mounted shift lever, standard "H" pattern. Synchronizers in 2nd and direct. *Synchro-Smooth Drive* (std. with Challenger, Challenger Special V-8's). Synchronized manual shifting in all forward gears; clash-free downshifting to low while under way. Floor-mounted stick.

4-Speed Manual (opt.)—sports-type close-ratio transmission, synchronized in all forward gears; floor-mounted stick.

CRUISE-O-MATIC DRIVE: (opt. except 271-hp V-8)—3-speed automatic with two selective drive ranges: 3-speed range starting in low for all normal driving; 2-speed range starting in intermediate for more sure-footed driving on slippery surfaces. Floor-mounted T-bar selector with sequence: P-R-N-DRIVE-L.

FRONT SUSPENSION: Angle-Poised Ball-Joint type with coil springs mounted on upper arms. 36,000-mile (or 3-year) lube intervals. Strut-stabilized lower arms. Link-type, rubber-bushed ride stabilizer. Built-in anti-dive control.

REAR SUSPENSION: Longitudinal, 4-leaf springs with rubber-bushed front mounts, compression-type shackles at rear. Asymmetrical, variable-rate design with rear axle located forward of spring centers for anti-squat on takeoff. Diagonally mounted shock absorbers.

REAR AXLE: Semi-floating hypoid rear axle; straddle-mounted drive pinion (V-8's). Permanently lubricated wheel bearings.

STEERING: Recirculating ball-type steering gear provides easy handling. Permanently lubricated steering linkage joints. Overall steering ratio 27 to 1 (power steering 22 to 1). Turning diameter 38 ft.

BRAKES: Self-adjusting, self-energizing design. Composite drums, grooved for extra cooling: 9-in. (Six), 10-in. (V-8's). Total lining area: 131 sq. in. (Six), 154 sq. in. (V-8's). Caliper-type front disc brakes optional.

TIRES: Tubeless, blackwall with Tyrex rayon cord, 4-ply rating. Safety-type rims. Tire size: with Six—6.50 x 13 (optional 6.95 x 14); with V-8's—6.95 x 14.

DIMENSIONS AND CAPACITIES: Overall length 181.6"; height 51.1"; width 68.2"; wheelbase 108"; treads—front 55.4" (Six), 56" (V-8), rear 56"; weight (approx.) 2621 lb. (2+2), 2562 lb. (Hardtop), 2740 lb. (Convertible); fuel 16 gal.; oil 4.5 qt. (Six), 5 qt. (V-8); cooling system (with heater) 9.5 qt. (Six), 14.5 qt. (V-8's); trunk luggage volume (cu. ft.): Hardtop 9, Convertible 7.7 (top down), Fastback 5 (18.5 trunk plus rear seat down).

PRICES: Mustang includes heater-defroster and front seat belts as standard equipment. However heater and/or seat belts may be deleted on car order if desired at an appropriate price reduction. All optional equipment and accessories, illustrated or referred to as options, optional or available are at extra cost. For the price of the Mustang with the equipment you desire, see your Ford Dealer.

EXTERIOR COLORS

	Code
Raven Black	A
Wimbleton White	M
Rangoon Red	J
Poppy Red	3
Silversmoke Gray	K
Silver Blue	Y
Caspian Blue	H
Tropical Turquoise	*O
Dynasty Green	D
Twilight Turquoise	*5
Ivy Green	*R
Champagne Beige	*I
Honey Gold	*C
Prairie Bronze	P
Sunlight Yellow	V
Vintage Burgandy	X

*These colors are new for 1965. Others are carried over from 1964½.

10 MUSTANG POWER TEAMS

ENGINES	TRANSMISSIONS
200 cu. in. Six*	A†, C, D
Challenger V-8	B†, C, D
Challenger Special V-8	B†, C, D
Challenger High Performance V-8	D

Standard Equipment Key:
*Engine (all models); †Transmissions (as indicated)
A—3-Speed Manual
B—Synchro-Smooth Drive (fully synchronized 3-speed manual)
C—Cruise-O-Matic Drive   **D**—4-Speed Manual

TWICE-A-YEAR MAINTENANCE: Mustangs are designed to go 6,000 miles (or 6 months) between oil changes and minor chassis lubrications; 36,000 miles (or 3 years, whichever comes first) between major chassis lubes. Other Mustang service savings: 36,000-mile (or 2-year) engine coolant-antifreeze, self-adjusting brakes; long-life Sta-Ful battery, sealed alternator, rust- and corrosion-resistant aluminized muffler; galvanized vital underbody parts. Mustang needs so little service it's just good sense to see that it gets the best—at your Ford Dealer's. His factory-trained mechanics and special tools add up to a great service combination you can get *nowhere* else!

NEW CAR WARRANTY: Throughout Mustang is *total-car* quality which makes possible this *total-car* warranty: Ford Motor Company warrants to owners as follows: That for 24 months or for 24,000 miles (3 months or 4,000 miles on Challenger High Performance V-8 engine and related power train components), whichever comes first, free replacement, including related labor, will be made by Ford Dealers of any part with a defect in workmanship or material. Tires are not covered by the warranty; appropriate adjustments will be made by tire companies. Owners will remain responsible for normal maintenance services, routine replacement of parts, such as filters, spark plugs, ignition points, wiper blades, brake and clutch linings, and normal deterioration of soft trim and appearance items. The warranty referred to herein is applicable to products sold in the U.S.A. and in certain neighboring areas.

Best year yet to go Ford
Test Drive Total Performance '65

MUSTANG · FALCON · FAIRLANE · FORD · THUNDERBIRD

1965 Mustang Convertible   *Bruce Williams, Oceanside, California*

1965 Mustang Hardtop

1965 Mustang 2+2 Fastback   *Charles Kitchell,*
San Diego, California

Tom McRae, Carlsbad, California

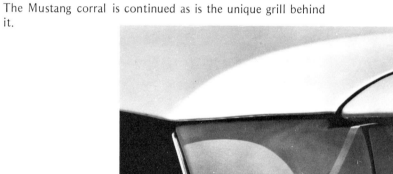

The overall appearance of the front end is essentially identical to the 1964½ model.

The Mustang corral is continued as is the unique grill behind it.

The forward corners of the 1965 hood have lost the "skirt" found earlier (page 33), and are now folded sharply under.

Parking lights are continued unchanged.

A "windsplit" crease extends the length of the hood.

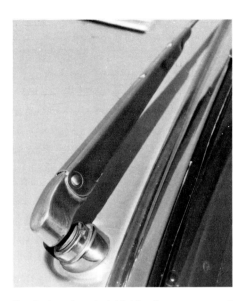

Dual electric windshield wipers are standard; two-speed wipers are an option at extra cost.

Air enters the heater plenum chamber through this grill at the base of the windshield.

The Vehicle Identification Number continues to appear on the left siderail where it may be seen when hood is raised.

The steel hood is mounted on spring-counterbalanced hinges and no support is required when it is raised.

The Mustang Hardtop and Fastback 2+2 bodies are all-steel welded structures which, when seam-welded to the under-body platform provide great rigidity. Special under-body reinforcements are required for the Convertible body which lacks this feature.

Body-side panels of the Convertible and the Hardtop are identical. Doors may be interchanged, although window frames differ.

Well-designed to appear as one piece, the grill ornament is actually composed of several parts. In addition to the Mustang itself, the center and lower bars can also be detached from the corral.

The one-piece cast "MUS-TANG" on the sides of the fenders are slightly longer than they were on 1964½ models. Now measuring almost 5" over-all, they are about ¼" longer than the earlier style (page 35).

The new Fastback 2+2 model has its name added to its fender side emblem.

As part of a special option an accenting paint stripe and rocker panel mouldings replace standard quarter panel trim.

The rocker panel moulding is standard on the 2+2 models, but an extra-cost option on the other two where it can be had either with the quarter panel trim strip or with an accent paint stripe.

53

A single wide door on each side allows access to front or rear seats. Quarter windows, which may be opened for ventilation, are standard on Hardtop and Convertible, but are not furnished on Fastback 2+2 models.

Vent windows on all models may be manually opened, and although the Hardtop and the Fastback 2+2 share similar windshield corner posts, that on the Convertible (left) is concealed by bright metal trim.

The push-button door handles are continued.

All glass is Tempered Safety Glass, including the vent windows.

The pattern on the door panel is unchanged.

Concealed switches in the two door jambs operate courtesy lights.

The Ford insignia is displayed again on the door sill.

The vinyl-covered standard arm rests continue and are again mounted on chromed plastic brackets.

The inside door lock knobs are now chromed, and a change has been made in the window outer weather-strip which now has a stainless steel backing (prior to September of 1964, it had a black beading).

Earlier style handles are secured with a C-clip behind skirt.

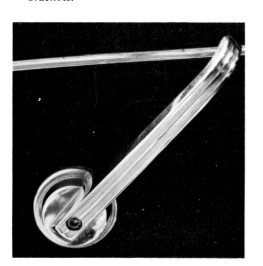

A running change finds the inside door latch and window riser handles modified to accept a mounting screw at their hub.

The Hardtop rear window is a wide curved section of Tempered Safety Glass.

Dress-up vinyl roof covering is offered as an option on the Hardtop in either black or white vinyl. A chromed trim strip is installed at the base of the roof.

A foam-lined Convertible top boot is standard and matches the 5-ply vinyl-bonded top. Available colors include Black, White or Tan.

Easy-action top clamps are provided to secure the folded Convertible top, but are omitted when Power Top option is ordered.

The doors of the Fastback 2+2 interchange with those of the other models although the windows do not. The shape of its roof substantially changes the appearance of the car and the slope of the window frame is deceptive.

The visible portion of the new Silent-Flo Ventiliation system provides a dramatic new styling feature.

Only on the Fastback 2+2 does this rear corner curve so sharply. That on the Hardtop (page 111) is quite square; Convertibles almost so.

Inside, a sliding control knob opens a concealed shutter in the ventilator.

Separate chromed exit grills are placed behind the louvers.

Courtesy lights are built into the rear sidewalls of the Fastback 2+2 and operated by switches in the doors.

The new Fastback 2+2 features a folding rear seat. In this position it provides minimal seating space for two passengers.

Rests are installed at the back corners of the compartment for the seat back.

With the rear seat back folded, a 35 x 41 inch storage platform emerges.

A single sliding latch is provided on the right rear quarter to secure the seat back in the erect position.

The rear panel can be released by a catch in the luggage compartment and folded up where it becomes a package shelf and extends the storage space into the trunk.

The wide rear window of the Fastback 2+2 is ten square feet of tinted glass.

The small luggage storage compartment of the Fastback 2+2 is almost filled by its spare tire.

A sliding catch in the luggage compartment releases the rear panel, and a latching support arm (seen behind tire) swings up with it as a support.

Back-up lights continue to be an extra-cost option on the 1965 Mustangs.

The rear deck lid of the Hardtop and the Convertible are interchangable, but a shorter lid is used on the Fastback 2+2 (previous page).

The external metal bezel suggests three separate tail lights although the lens is one single piece.

The lid is secured by a keylock.

The gas cap is secured with a protective wire loop and bolted to the car.

The sporty standard bucket seats are complimented by color-keyed steering wheel, now also available in a sixth color, Palomino. *Padded* sun visors are an extra cost option.

The horn-blowing steering wheel spider is one piece and the "holes" are painted depressions.

Mustang name is continued on the spider's hub.

This Deluxe Seat Belt, complete with retractors, is available at extra cost.

The individually adjustable front seats are upholstered in either all-vinyl, or (in the Hardtop and Fastback 2+2) in cloth and vinyl combination. Front seat belts are standard.

The console suggests an enclosure of the bucket seats, another "sporty" touch.

The full-length console, an option in the other models, was initially standard in the new 1965 Fastback 2+2 which also featured color-keyed headliners and standard padded sun visors.

Installation of a console calls for the replacement of the standard (page 139) shift indicator unit with a flat assembly which includes a sliding dust-plate around the shift lever.

The rear seat assemblies of the Hardtop (left) and Convertible (above) are alike. Convertible, however, includes standard ash trays in the rear panels while none are furnished in the Coupe or Fastback 2+2.

Standard instrument panel padding extends over the panel in protective fashion.

The OFF position of the heater fan switch is now placed to the left rather than centered as previously.

An AM radio is offered as an option. When not ordered, a blanking plate (page 124) is provided.

A narrow chrome trim strip dresses up the lower edge of the instrument panel padding.

The control knob on the left-side incoming air vent is now plain, not lettered as it was in earlier models.

The pad dips smoothly over the radio.

1965

This is the last year for the horizontal speedometer scale which was initially adapted from the earlier Falcon unit. In the Spring of 1965, a new five-dial instrument panel appears with the new GT option (page 99) and is carried over on all 1966 models.

Above the OIL warning light is an illuminated headlight high-beam indicator.

A change under the hood finds an alternator replacing the earlier DC generators. Thus, the charging circuit warning lamp now reads ALT in place of the earlier GEN. At the end of the speedometer scale appears an illuminated turn signal lamp.

Single-speed electric wipers are standard, but an extra-cost option is available featuring two-speed wipers.

Cigarette lighter is standard equipment, as is the heater-defroster.

The parking brake handle is unchanged and continues to be suspended under the left side of the instrument panel.

This is the standard foot pedal supplied when the vehicle is equipped with the optional Cruise-O-Matic drive (available with all except the 271 horsepower optional High Performance engine). Brakes are self-adjusting internal-expanding type. Front disc brakes are optional accessories.

In February of 1962, some two years *before* the public introduction of the new Ford Mustang, a group headed by Carroll Shelby, retired race car driver, assembled the first of what later would become possibly the world's most mis-identified automobile in the back room of a hospitable Automotive Equipment manufacturer's facility in Santa Fe Springs, California.

The Cobra, as Shelby called the car (it has since been claimed that the name occurred to him in a dream) was a Ford-engined vehicle derived from an AC Cars Ltd. two-seated sports car. Cobra is properly the name by which this Shelby car is designated, but the name later became the property of Ford and not only was used to designate the 1968 Mustang-based Shelby models, then the bigger Ford Torino Cobras, and later was again used on certain models of the Mustang II.

A well-engineered assembly of the domestic Ford 289 V-8 engine (later also the larger 427 cid was used) shoehorned into the lightweight AC chassis and body, *Cobra* was a sturdy and formidable competitor. Initially designed for use with a 6-cylinder Bristol engine, AC's tubular steel chassis and light-weight aluminum body nevertheless proved to be essentially sturdy enough for this job. With appropriate re-engineering of structural elements, Shelby-American's product succeeded in establishing itself as a "super-car" in short order and the name grew in significance. Thus, even contemporary Mustang-based Shelby cars are frequently called "Cobras", but strictly speaking, they are not, despite the use of the word in describing its engine.

Incorporating in March of 1962 as Shelby-American, Incorporated, the group moved to its own facility in Venice, another Los Angeles suburb, in June and by August they showed their prototype. Entering the racing circuits, the *Cobra* attracted attention as it succeeded in winning the United States Road Racing Championship in 1963 (and again in 1964) as well as six consecutive Sports Car Club of America National Championships from 1963 on, defeating Corvettes, Ferraris, Porsches and others.

By the late Fall of 1963, Shelby-American was working on an even faster aerodynamically superior, enclosed body model, and in February of 1964 they introduced their "Daytona Coupe", an extremely low-production version which participated with the roadster in bringing *Cobra* the FIA World Championship in 1965.

Through 1964, Shelby-American was successfully assembling AC-bodied Ford-powered *Cobra* sports cars at their Venice facility, and by now Ford had introduced its new Mustang.

In early advertisement, Cobra is touted as having a top speed of 175 miles per hour and capable of 0-60 mph in 4.2 seconds!

Since an identification with the race-winning *Cobra* sports car would add to the already-exciting Mustang image, it became logical to investigate an association that would profit both Ford and Shelby-American.

With the readily available Ford bolt-on accessory Total Performance Options added to Mustang's already potent High Performance Engine Option (together with its necessary Special Handling Package), all that was really necessary was for someone knowledgeable to put together the packages. While it is undoubtedly true that Ford's own people could probably have done this, the press of other obligations prevented them from doing it, and Shelby-American was selected to modify Ford's Mustang into an even more roadworthy competitor. Thus, the GT-350 was born.

When no better suggestion appeared, in another flash of reported intuition, this car is alleged to have been named by Carroll Shelby "for the estimated distance between the Competition and the Production Shops at Shelby-American". The name does not appear to have any other significance, and is unrelated to horsepower, cubic inches, or other specific dimensions, so this claim is likely true.

Surviving 289 Cobra races across Wisconsin flatlands in 1977 photograph.

A formidible competitor, the aggressive new GT-350 won with ease, gaining the Sports Car Club of America National Championship in 1965, then again in 1966 and 1967. Racing in B Production (the name related to comparative performance potential, and is not derogatory), it defeated Feraris, Corvettes, Jaguar XK-E, Lotus and Mercedes-Benz 300SL with ease. Not only a new sports car was born, even a new merchandising strategy emerged. Buyers could purchase a car right off the floor, use it for "ordinary" transportation, and race the same car at weekend competitions! Surprisingly, Hertz Rental (see page 90) placed almost one thousand such cars in their inventory in 1966 for the Renter who fancied himself a race car driver.

Shelby-American moved into larger quarters in rented hangers at the Los Angeles airport in March of 1965 where they continued the production of

The Cobra Daytona Coupe, together with the Cobra Roadster, produced outstanding wins in 1965 for the FIA World's Manufacturer's Championship.

both their Cobra and their newer GT-350. Continuing the simultaneous production of the Cobra, Shelby commenced the production of the 1967 289 powered GT-350 and the new 428-engined GT-500 there in October of 1966, but in March of 1967 they assembled their last Cobra. Later, in August, assembly of the Mustang-based cars was transferred to another entity, Shelby-Automotive, in Ironia, Michigan where Ford assumed more control over production and where more fiberglass parts suppliers were available.

1968 models were designated as "Shelby Cobras", by Ford, and the name Cobra then dropped for these cars until it was revived in 1975 on the Mustang II. Production of the "Shelbys" continued with the 1969 Model and some few hold-over cars were sold as 1970 models, after which time the name was laid to rest.

Carroll Shelby, entrepreneur, whose charisma had brought it all together, continues his interests. In 1977, one Company in which he has an interest is re-manufacturing the distinctive Shelby-American wheels; another offers Performance Parts, and yet another is aggressively merchandising a tasty Texas-Style chili mix.

Cobras were exciting additions to contemporary motion pictures. In SPINOUT, a 1966 MGM release, Cecil Kellaway and Una Merkle wish the late Elvis Presley good luck with his 427 Cobra.

The Shelby GT 350 was built both for Street and for Track. In the foreground is a street version dressed up with optional Shelby aluminum wheels. Beside it is the race-ready competition version.

1965 GT 350

Interior of Shelby American competition shop. The cars, as delivered from Ford's San Jose Assembly Plant had conventional steel wheels. Shelby's only 1965 option (at extra cost) was a set of special racing type wheels.

Photo from Shelby American Press Release

The GT 350 had an altered front geometry to improve cornering. As cars passed down production line, workers in pit lowered the upper A-frame mounting (photo page 70) installed heavier front stabilizer, heavy duty Koni shock absorbers, finned aluminum oil pan, tuned exhaust headers, and dress-up valve covers (lower right).

Photo from Shelby American Press Release

1965 Shelby-American GT 350 *Larry Zane, Swedesboro, New Jersey*

The first Shelby GT 350, produced early in October of 1964, is serial number SFM (for Shelby-Ford-Mustang) #5R001, and the car has now been restored to the condition it was in when raced originally. A fully race-prepared vehicle, it represents the initial thinking at Shelby-American in regard to producing a truly competitive automobile. The street versions (page 76), production of which commenced only weeks later, are tamer by far than this all-out competition vehicle.

A special nameplate bearing the Shelby serial number is riveted over the Ford-stamped VIN numbers on the left frame-rail and can be seen when the hood is raised. (Ford's serial numbers would commence "5R09K" on all genuine GT 350s).

The GT 350 competition model is fitted with a fibre-glass lower front valance with a wide cut-out to improve airflow through radiator. Holes to either side are intakes for front brake cooling ducts.

The number "61" refers to the entry number this particular car wore when raced in 1965/66 by the Shelby team.

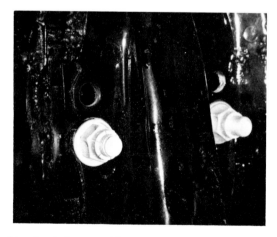

Steering is improved in turns by lowering the front wheel upper control arms one inch.

The conventional Mustang grill insignia is omitted, and a new aluminum lower grill center trim provided on the GT 350.

To stiffen front end, Shelby adds the "Monte Carlo" bar, so-named for its initial use earlier on Falcons raced there, across the shock absorber towers and the "export" brace, a one-piece stiffener from cowl to towers is substituted for the conventional Mustang two-piece stampings.

The dual wide "Le Mans" stripes used by Shelby American on their race entries were not supplied on the GT 350 street cars. Buyers, who often wanted these attractive decorative stripes could have them installed by the selling Dealers.

Headlights were generally taped before racing to prevent danger of flying glass.

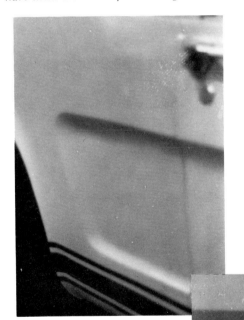

A side scoop appears on the left side (only) of GT 350 #5R001. Contrary to popular belief, this scoop was not related to brake cooling air, but was intended as an inlet for a rear-end (differential) lubricant cooling system. Although this system proved unnecessary and was abandoned, the scoop was never removed.

Race-prepared GT 350 cars were provided with these special 15 inch wheels and Goodyear high speed racing tires made especially for Shelby American.

The rear glass of the Mustang was removed and a new plastic window replaces it in the competition cars. A slight space is allowed at the top to draw air out of the driver's compartment and thus ventilate it.

The conventional Fastback 2+2 rear quarter grill assembly is removed to save weight and a sheet aluminum panel pop-riveted in its place on competition models.

Behind the larger 1" front anti-sway bar which has replaced a smaller standard Mustang stabilizer bar can be seen the special Cobra oil pan which features a larger capacity oil sump.

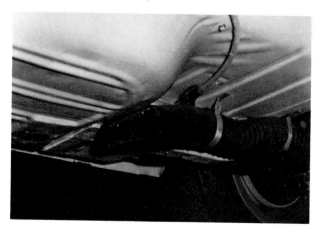

Rear brakes are additionally cooled on the competition cars by means of a duct system installed under the car.

Commencing in 1965, Shelby offered almost all of the GT 350 parts "over the counter" for those wishing to improve or modify the performance of stock Mustangs. These included, among other items, headers, oil pans, manifolds, hoods, side scoops, as well as complete engines and engine components.

An English "Raydyot" racing mirror is used on the competition cars (the street car mirror appears on page 80).

Mustang's side window assembly is discarded and replaced with a welded-aluminum frame with plastic windows to save weight on race-prepared cars. The replacement vent window will not open, but the side windows can be lowered.

Unnecessary weight is eliminated on competition cars by removing the window riser assembly and arm rests.

Padding protects the driver's elbow.

A webbed strap with press fasteners is furnished to adjust the position of the side windows in competition cars.

A Stewart-Warner electric fuel pump mounted in the rear compartment aids in getting fuel to the engine.

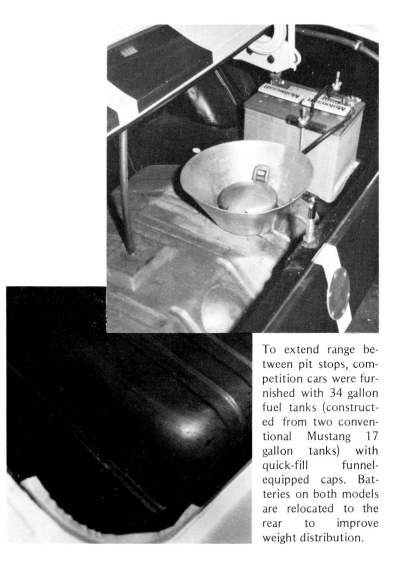

To extend range between pit stops, competition cars were furnished with 34 gallon fuel tanks (constructed from two conventional Mustang 17 gallon tanks) with quick-fill funnel-equipped caps. Batteries on both models are relocated to the rear to improve weight distribution.

Deck lid latching mechanism is replaced by a locking pin, and the hole in the rear panel for the conventional fuel filler tube closed by a blanking plate,

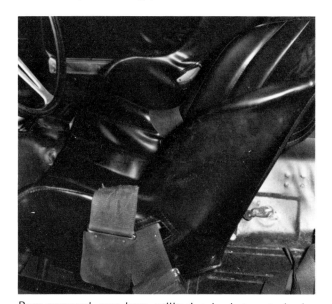

Race-prepared cars have utilitarian bucket seats having almost no padding, and are equipped with competition type seat belts.

Interior of the competition car is gutted to save weight, and the required spare wheel is mounted on a fibre-glass panel which replaces the conventional folding rear seat of Mustang's Fastback 2+2.

Race-prepared cars are provided with a new instrument panel replacing the conventional Mustang unit entirely. Gauges indicate (from left) Fuel Pressure, Oil Temperature, Speed, Engine RPM, Oil Pressure, and Water Temperature.

A 160 mph speedometer is provided in the competition cars, its face bearing the Shelby C/S emblem as do the other instruments.

The tachometer is rotated, not to place its red-line position in a more visible position, but because of a mechanical interference behind the panel.

A three-spoked wood-and-aluminum racing type steering wheel replaces the conventional Mustang steering wheel. Although it lacks a horn button, its value lies in placing the driver's hands at a better angle due to a somewhat flatter shape.

Although the panels are pierced for them, radios are not standard equipment, and since they are certainly not required for racing, are omitted in competition cars. To the left of opening can be seen the switch provided for sounding the horn.

G.T. 350

Mustang, competition-modified by Carroll Shelby. The brilliant new fastback GT/350 is a top performer. Hand assembled in Southern California in limited quantities by the craftsmen who are responsible for the championship Ford-powered Cobra sports car, the GT/350 represents the finest combination of sports car performance with stock car practicality. Offering racing car suspension, disc brakes, 15" wheels, performance-tuned 289 Cobra engine, limited-slip rear end and race-bred interior, the GT/350 is designed for the individual who wants the finest in performance. Write direct to GT/350, c/o Shelby American, 6501 West Imperial Highway, Los Angeles, California 90009.

JUNE, 1965

The street version of the 1965 Shelby American GT 350 was, of course, the true "production" model. Containing most, but not all, of the modifications made to the race-prepared cars, it was a strong contender and a rugged aggressive automobile.

Fewer eliminations of the standard Mustang's comforts were made; side windows and rear windows remained unchanged, and Mustang's far more comfortable front bucket seats, and fuel system were standard, but handling and engine changes followed the competition car. All had Koni shock absorbers, the Detroit Locker rear end, larger rear brakes (taken from Ford's Galaxie line), and, for tighter steering, special pitman and idler arms.

562 1965 Mustang Fastback 2+2 units were converted into the GT 350 by Shelby American and about 240 more were held over and retitled as 1966 cars. All were painted Wimbleton White and had black vinyl interiors. A surprisingly large number of these cars have survived; according to a recently published survey, the whereabouts of over 200 1965 GT 350's have been established.

1965 Shelby-American GT 35

1965 GT 350

Mr. Robert Key, Laguna Hills, California

1965 GT 350

Hood pins replace the conventional adjustable rests (page 32), and the Mustang latching mechanism assembly is deleted for further weight savings.

Early 1965 GT 350 hoods are fibre-glass for lighter weight (later in the year they were steel-reinforced). To prevent warping these light-weight hoods, the hinge springs are removed.

Changes were made in the engine compartment of the standard Mustang. In addition to relocating the battery to the rear, these included the use of heavy-duty radiators built to Shelby American specifications and a heavy-duty master brake cylinder. With the improved breathing, larger carburetor, and overall tuning, the already-high performance 289 engine was providing over 300 horsepower. Behind the engine, a close-ratio Borg-Warner T-10 aluminum-cased transmission replaced the heavier Ford four-speed transmission.

The GT 350 hood has a built-in, largely decorative, air scoop. Hoods, and even scoops, were sold by Shelby American for use as dress-up accessories on conventional Mustangs.

Street model has conventional lower front valance, not cut-out style used on competition versions (page 70).

At the left side of the GT 350 radiator grill can be found the standard Mustang insignia used on the front fenders of that car.

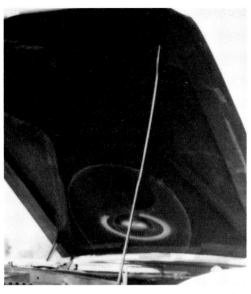

A hinged hood prop is supplied to hold the non-counterbalanced hoop open.

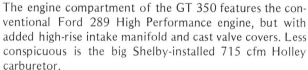

The engine compartment of the GT 350 features the conventional Ford 289 High Performance engine, but with added high-rise intake manifold and cast valve covers. Less conspicuous is the big Shelby-installed 715 cfm Holley carburetor.

15" steel wheels were standard, but as their only option Shelby-American offered these attractive five-spoke Aluminum wheels. All cars were fitted with 130 mph Goodyear "Blue Dot" tires.

In addition to riveting their Identification Plate to the car, Shelby-American took the precaution of *also* stamping their own number directly into the right-side frame rail.

The Shelby-American nameplate continues to be installed directly over the Ford-stamped VIN on the left frame rail. Registration, for title purposes, is based on the Shelby number.

79

Tubular steel "double Wye" headers (page 134) and straight-through glass packed mufflers, installed by Shelby American, end in a short exhaust pipe curved sharply out the sides just ahead of the rear wheels.

A Talbot-type chromed side view mirror is used on the street model. This option is dealer-installed.

The lettering is formed of 3-M contact tape, and the stripes are painted to match, explaining the slight difference in tint.

The orientation of the stripes finds the bottom edge of the center stripe placed just below the door sill.

The radio and antenna are a Dealer-installed accessory. Since the fiber-glass hood will not shield ignition interference, the antenna is mounted at the rear.

The accessory LeMans stripes are Dealer-installed, and match the standard side-stripes.

The early 1965 GT 350 was equipped with a standard 1965 Mustang gas cap, and generally had a rectangular nameplate added near the right rear tail light.

Late 1965 models had a special Shelby insignia gas cap which carried over onto the 1966 models, and frequently lacked the nameplate near the taillight.

1965 GT 350

Steering wheels with both "slotted spokes" and others with "pierced spokes" are both correct and appear to have been used indiscriminately by the factory.

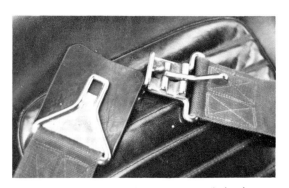

The standard competition-type seat belts have a positive latch.

The street models of GT 350 have conventional Mustang interiors as furnished by the factory, and are not modified to save weight as are the race-prepared models.

A fiber-glass tray replaces the rear seat assembly of the Mustang Fastback 2+2 and the spare tire is removed from the luggage compartment and mounted here. Rear panel is "dished" to accommodate the tire.

The somewhat more comfortable Mustang standard bucket seats remain unchanged in the GT 350.

This door sill plate is fastened over the conventional Ford insignia (page 37).

A bezel containing a tachometer and an oil pressure unit is added at top center of the instrument panel, blending nicely with it. Both instrument faces bear the C/S insignia. Installation of the pressure unit required the addition of an oil pressure sensing line from the engine as the standard instrument panel only contained warning lights.

The appearance of the steering wheel hub is improved by the addition of a cap bearing the Cobra insignia. However, the horn is still activated by a switch placed on the instrument panel.

Continuing the 15" wheels on the "left-over 1965" 1966 GT 350, the cars beginning with those based on the 1966 Mustang were equipped with standard 14" wheels. Gray, Magnum 500, (chromed on the GT 350H) wheels were standard and Shelby-American offered additionally a new 10-spoke magnesium alloy wheel as an option.

1965 models had been available only in Wimbleton White and this continued initially but later options included Guardsman Blue, Candy Apple Red, Ivy Green, and Raven Black.

1966 Shelby American GT 350

1966 GT 350

Shelby American had built 562 1965 GT 350 cars and held over an additional approximately 240 which were retitled as 1966 models. These, obviously, were essentially the same. Then, starting with about the 240th 1966 car, the basis was the 1966 Mustang and thus later cars had _its_ features.

Over 2300 1966 GT 350 vehicles, including some 936 GT 350H Hertz models, (and six Convertibles), were produced by the end of September of 1966.

A dramatic change occurred in the appearance of the 1966 GT 350 with the addition of see-through plastic quarter windows and rear brake cooling air scoops.

Mr. Z. Z. DePriest, San Diego, California

1966 GT 350

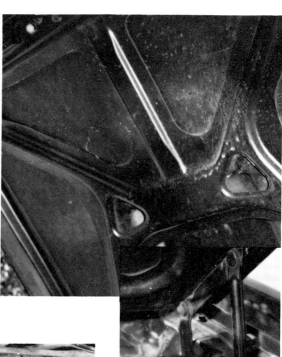

Late in 1965, construction of GT 350 hoods was altered and they received steel reinforcements (right) under the fiber-glass. Hood pins (left) were retained for appearance, as the conventional Mustang latching mechanism remained.

Hood hinge springs were retained on the 1966 cars.

This is the Mustang hood latch mechanism. It was removed from early GT 350 units, but left intact on the 1966 models.

Few obvious changes appear in the 1966 GT 350 engine compartment. During 1966, Shelby stopped lowering the front A-frame pivots (page 70).

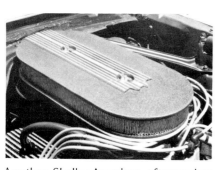

Another Shelby-American after-market item was a Dual 4-V High Riser Induction Kit, with two 460 cfm carburetors, linkage, and air cleaner, which first appeared late in 1966.

Starting in 1966, Shelby-American offered a full line of after-market performance parts. Among them was this racing radiator.

Mustang cooling is aided by shrouding the fan for venturi effect. The part, frequently discarded by radiator rebuilders, is retained on the GT 350.

This side view mirror, Dealer-installed option, is sold under a standard Ford (Rotunda) part number.

New narrower side stripe assembly is placed higher on the sides adding to apparent length. Blue stripes are used on white cars, white stripes on the others (except Hertz).

The 1966 side stripe is all-tape, and slightly shorter in height. It's lower edge is placed just *above* the bottom of the door (compare page 80).

Most striking change for 1966 is the addition of plastic windows in place of the blanking plates used on 1965 models.

For 1966, scoops are added, with functional internal ducts to direct cooling air to the rear brake system.

Above is an original embossed 1966 Shelby-American door sill plate. Below is the painted replacement part.

Exhaust tips now exit beneath the rear bumper, a change made to reduce cockpit noise.

1966 Mustangs have standard back-up lights, and these find their way to the later GT 350 which is based on these cars.

The GT 350 Cobra gas cap, introduced during 1965, is continued through 1966.

The GT 350 nameplate continues near the right rear taillight.

Initially, Shelby-American continued to relocate the battery to the rear, but shortly after commencing work on the 1966 models, the plan was abandoned and the battery retained under the hood.

Traction bars, a mechanical parallelogram, employed to reduce axle "hop" under heavy acceleration, had been installed on the GT 350 from the start. Initially installed *over* the rear axle, their forward upper ends protruded into the passenger compartment. Later, on the 1966 models, they were redesigned and installed *below* the axle. Koni shock absorbers, standard in 1965, were options in 1966 and the standard Ford heavy-duty shocks thus often appear.

The optional accessory Mustang Deluxe Steering Wheel is standard on the 1966 GT 350, and the horn can now be operated at the spokes.

These 1966 GT 350 Cobra tachometers are mounted on the instrument panels of different cars. Serving the same purpose, there seems to be no explanation for the slight differences in their appearance.

Automatic transmissions became increasingly popular in the 1966 GT 350. When furnished, they were the conventional Ford C-4 automatic transmission, and cars were equipped with smaller Ford 460 cfm carburetors and softer, power-assisted, brakes.

Rear seat assemblies were allegedly removed, and for the demanding buyer, could be "reinstalled" for the sum of $75. Most 1966 models were produced with the seat intact.

Another of Shelby-American's late 1966 aftermarket accessories is this Competition Roll Bar, designed to be welded directly to the frame.

1966 GT 350H

In an unusually successful approach to the Hertz Rental System, Shelby-American was able to secure an order for 1000 of the 1966 GT 350 to be placed by Hertz at many of their Rental Agencies. These cars continued to feature most of the GT 350 features in order to attract the renter who fancied himself a member of the racing fraternity. However, the cars also had to meet practical commercial considerations, and thus varied in some respects. Example—speedometer cable locks were used to prevent tampering with mileage. Most had radios, and softer brake systems were provided for the general public.

Nine hundred and thirty-six of these cars were produced for Hertz, and after serving in their fleet, these cars were re-sold. Representing, as they do, almost 40% of Shelby-American's 1966 production, they are an important part of that Company's history.

1966 Shelby-American GT 350H

Mr. James Sentivan, Westfield, New Jersey

photo by William S. Jackson

91

1966 GT 350H

Hertz GT 350H models were delivered in Raven Black, Wimbleton White, Guardsman Blue, Ivy Green, and Candy Apple Red. All had Gold Bronze body stripes and side stripes.

The Hertz cars have an all-steel hood, similar in appearance to the GT 350 hoods. Some of these all-steel hoods were used on very late 1966 GT 350 models.

Stripe pattern continues from front lip of the hood up to the base of the windshield.

Standard Hertz gold side stripes match the LeMans body stripes in color.

Both the GT 350 and the Hertz GT 350H models continue to use the Mustang fender ornament on their grills.

Hertz cars, like other GT 350 units, have rear exhaust.

A conventional GT 350 Cobra gas cap is used on the Hertz cars, as is the GT 350 nameplate. No special "GT 350H" identifications are used except on the side stripe.

These window assemblies used on the 1966 GT 350 cars, are plastic, not glass.

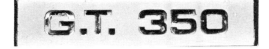

1966 GT 350H

The Deluxe Steering Wheel option of the 1966 Mustang is the standard steering wheel for the Hertz GT 350H cars. This car is missing its panel-mounted tachometer (seen below).

Competition-type seat belts are provided in the front seats.

This is an optional accessory wood-rimmed stainless steel steering wheel offered by Shelby-American for their GT 350's. Included is a Cobra-emblemed horn button. The instrument panel-mounted tachometer is standard, but the air conditioner is an after-market Ford accessory.

By mid 1966, a tamer GT 350 was emerging, a car less virile and aggressive than originally planned. No longer the all-out road-eating race machine, it retained its competitive reputation, but started losing its more exotic refinements.

Front end suspension changes, considered necessary initially, including lowering the upper arm pivot points, were omitted; weight-transferring battery and spare wheel relocations no longer considered necessary; over-the-axle traction bars relocated beneath the axle, Detroit Locker rear end made optional, and most visibly, the Mustang folding rear seat and automatic transmission was appearing in more and more of the Shelby-American cars.

Rear-seat passengers have excellent visibility with Shelby-American's new plastic window inserts.

Door sill plates used in later 1966 production had added "los angeles, california" to the simpler style used earlier (page 87).

Although competition-type seat belts are provided in front, standard Mustang seat belts remain in the rear.

The fold-down rear seat, a $75 Shelby-American option, was furnished in virtually all 1966 GT 350H models and most 1966 GT 350 cars as well.

MUSTANG GT

Ford's new GT option was introduced in April of 1965 as a late-model year dress-up option. Relating the concept to their currently successful all-out GT racing machine, Ford sought to transfer some of that vehicle's charisma, as well possibly as that of the GT 350, to their production Mustang line where the GT option was offered on all three body styles. The attempt was successful and over 15,000 late-1965 Mustang buyers opted for the GT package and in 1966, almost 30,000 more purchased the option.

The GT Option transformed the car into a "Mustang GT" by adding performance options, also available separately, such as the 225 horse-power 4-v V-8 engine (the 271 hp High Performance engine was a further option on the GT package), heavy-duty suspension, front disc brakes, 3-speed fully synchronized transmission (Cruise-O-Matic and 4-speed transmissions were also additional options), with attractive dress-up kits. These included the front fog light assembly, special side stripes, and a dual exhaust system terminating in special GT exhaust trumpets.

Ford's market preferred the luxury of the Mustang GT with its modified performance features to the relatively Spartan but more competitive GT 350. Although the path of these two variants would tend to converge, eventually both would be dropped and succeeded by other marques such as the Mach 1 and the fabulous Boss cars.

Interesting fog lamps are a GT feature (although sold separately as well) and are operated by a switch placed at the left side of the instrument panel. The chrome hood lip moulding, introduced as part of the GT package, became standard on all 1966 Mustangs.

1965 Mustang GT Convertible

A GT emblem replaces the conventional Mustang unit, the name spelled out in individual letters, and a vinyl body stripe added on the lower sides of the cars equipped with the GT Option.

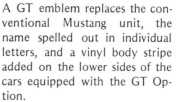

Initially furnished with the standard 1965 gas cap, this attractive cap was introduced on the 1966 Mustang GT cars.

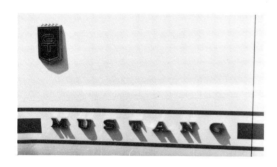

Mr. Fred Meyers, La Mesa, California

MUSTANG GT

This new five-dial Instrument Panel, which is mechanically interchanged with the earlier 1965 style (page 64) was introduced as a part of the GT Option and became standard for all 1966 Mustangs.

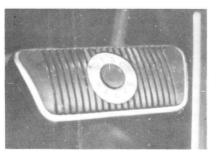

Front disc brakes, with special foot pedal, are part of the GT Option, along with the Special Handling Package which includes heavy-duty springs and shock absorbers and other steering modifications. Both items are also available separately as individual options.

The GT Option, available only with one of the two larger V-8 engines, not only has a dual-exhaust system, but also special exhaust "trumpets" which exit through holes in the special lower rear valance panel. The conventional rear bumper guards (page 60) are omitted on the GT models.

The "convertible brace", a pair of bars added from the cowl to the forward part of the side frame rails, first appeared on the GT Convertibles and were later added to all 1966 Convertibles. The stiffer bodies of the Hardtop and Fastback 2+2 do not require this reinforcement.

1966

1966 Exterior Paint Color Codes

Black	A
Light Blue	F
Light Beige	H
Dark Blue Metallic	*K
White	M
Medium Palomino Metallic	*P
Dark Ivy Green Metallic	R
Red	T
Medium Turquois Metallic	U
Emberglo Metallic	V
Maroon Metallic	X
Light Blue Metallic	Y
Medium Sage Gold Metallic	*Z
Medium Silver Metallic	4
Yellow	8

*new colors for 1966

1966 MUSTANG Specifications

11 MUSTANG POWER TEAMS

ENGINES	TRANSMISSIONS
200-cu. in. Six*	A†, C, D
Challenger V-8	B†, C, D
Challenger Special V-8	B†, C, D
Cobra V-8	C, D

STANDARD EQUIPMENT KEY:
*Engine (all models): †Transmissions (as indicated)

A—3-Speed Manual
B—Synchro-Smooth Drive (fully synchronized 3-speed manual)
C—Cruise-O-Matic Drive D—4-Speed Manual

COLOR AND UPHOLSTERY SELECTIONS: Pick your favorite color from 16 brilliant new Super Diamond Lustre Enamel single tones. Counting standard and optional choices, there are a total of 16 all-vinyl trims for the Hardtop, 2+2 and Convertible. Your Ford Dealer will be happy to show you actual samples of new Mustang colors and upholsteries.

ENGINES: ***120-hp Six*** (std.)—200-cu. in. displ.; 3.68" bore x 3.13" stroke; 9.2 to 1 comp. ratio; 7 main bearings; reg. fuel; single-barrel carb.; auto. choke; self-adj. valves with hydraulic lifters.

200-hp Challenger V-8 (opt.)—289-cu. in. displ.; 4.00" bore x 2.87" stroke; 9.3 to 1 comp. ratio; reg. fuel; 2-barrel carb.; auto. choke; self-adj. valves with hydraulic lifters.

225-hp Challenger Special V-8 (opt.)—289-cu. in. displ.; 4.00" bore x 2.87" stroke; 10.0 to 1 comp. ratio; 4-barrel carb.; prem. fuel. Other specifications same as Challenger V-8 above.

271-hp Cobra V-8 (opt.)—289-cu. in. displ.; 4.00" bore x 2.87" stroke; 10.5 to 1 comp. ratio; super prem. fuel; 4-barrel carb.; manual choke; solid valve lifters; dual exhaust.

ENGINE FEATURES: 6000-mile (or 6-month) full-flow disposable-type oil filter; replaceable dry element air cleaner; 190° thermostat; 12-volt electrical system with 38-amp. alternator; 42-amp. alternator on High Performance V-8; 54-plate, 45 amp-hr battery; weatherproof ignition; positive-engagement starter; fully aluminized muffler and tailpipe. All engines are electronically mass-balanced for long-lived smoothness.

Own a trailer? Planning to buy one? Your Ford Dealer can help you equip your new Mustang for many of the popular sizes The Mustang optional equipment suggestions listed here can add a great deal to smooth-sailing trailer trips with your Mustang.

MUSTANG TRAILER TOWING RECOMMENDATIONS: Class I (gross trailer weight up to 2,000 lb.; static tongue load up to 200 lb.)—200-hp V-8 or 225-hp V-8; Cruise-O-Matic Drive; extra cooling package; 6.95 x 14 4-ply rating tires; power steering and brakes; heavy-duty battery. For additional information, ask your Ford Dealer for a copy of the "1966 Ford Cars & Trucks for Recreation" brochure.

MANUAL TRANSMISSIONS: ***3-Speed Manual*** (std. with Six). Floor-mounted shift lever, standard "H" pattern. Synchronizers in 2nd and direct. ***Synchro-Smooth Drive*** (std. with Challenger, Challenger Special V-8's). Synchronized manual shifting in all three forward gears; clash-free downshifting to low while under way. Floor-mounted stick.

4-Speed Manual (opt.)—Sports-type close-ratio transmission, synchronized in all forward gears; floor-mounted stick.

CRUISE-O-MATIC DRIVE: (opt.)—3-speed automatic with two selective drive ranges; 3-speed range starting in low for all normal driving; 2-speed range starting in intermediate for more surefooted driving on slippery surfaces. Floor-mounted T-bar selector with sequence: P-R-N-DRIVE-L.

FRONT SUSPENSION: Angle-Poised Ball-Joint type with coil springs mounted on upper arms. 36,000-mile (or 3-year) lube intervals. Strut-stabilized lower arms. Link-type, rubber-bushed ride stabilizer.

REAR SUSPENSION: Longitudinal, 4-leaf springs with rubber-bushed front mounts, compression-type shackles at rear. Asymmetrical, variable-rate design with rear axle located forward of spring centers for anti-squat on takeoff. Diagonally mounted shock absorbers.

REAR AXLE: Semi-floating hypoid rear axle; straddle-mounted drive pinion (V-8's). Permanently lubricated wheel bearings.

STEERING: Recirculating ball-type steering gear provides easy handling. Permanently lubricated steering linkage joints. Overall steering ratio 27 to 1 (power steering 22 to 1). Turning diameter 38 ft.

BRAKES: Self-adjusting, self-energizing design. Composite drums grooved for extra cooling: 9" (Six), 10" (V-8's). Total lining areas: 131 sq. in. (Six), 154 sq. in. (V-8's). Front disc brakes optional.

TIRES: Tubeless, blackwall with Tyrex rayon cord, 4-ply rating. Safety-type rims. Tire size—6.95 x 14.

DIMENSIONS AND CAPACITIES: Overall length 181.6"; height 51.1"; width 68.2"; wheelbase 108"; treads—front 55.4" (Six), 56" (V-8), rear 56"; fuel 16 gal.; oil 4.5 qt. (Six), 5 qt. (V-8); cooling system (with heater) 9.5 qt. (Six) 14.5 qt. (V-8's); trunk luggage volume (cu. ft.): Hardtop 9, Convertible 7.7 (top down), Fastback 5 (18.5 trunk plus rear seat down).

PRICES: Mustang includes heater-defroster as standard equipment. However heater-defroster may be deleted on car order if desired at an appropriate price reduction. All optional equipment and accessories, illustrated or referred to as options, optional or available are at extra cost. For the price of the Mustang with the equipment you desire, see your Ford Dealer.

MUSTANG "WORTH MORE" FEATURES: In addition to all the new Mustang features you can read about in this catalog, there are many others which will make the 1966 Mustang you buy now more rewarding in both driving pleasure and resale value. Just a few of these "Worth More" features include: Safety-Yoke door latches, aluminum scuff plates, seat side shields, parallel-action electric windshield wipers, curved side glass, suspended accelerator, brake and clutch pedals, deep-dish design steering wheel with chrome horn ring, dual sun visors with retention clips, front arm rests, coat hooks, 2-position door checks, counterbalanced hood and rear deck lid and many, many more.

TWICE-A-YEAR MAINTENANCE: '66 Mustangs are designed to go 6,000 miles (or 6 months) between oil changes and minor chassis lubrications; 36,000 miles (or 3 years, whichever comes first) between major chassis lubes. Other Mustang service savings: 36,000-mile (or 2-year) engine coolant-antifreeze, self-adjusting brakes; long-life Sta-Ful battery, shielded alternator, rust- and corrosion-resistant aluminized muffler; galvanized vital underbody parts. Mustang needs so little service it's just good sense to see that it gets the best—at your Ford Dealer's. His factory-trained mechanics and special tools add up to the greatest service combination you'll ever find for your Mustang!

NEW CAR WARRANTY: Throughout Mustang is *total-car* quality which makes possible this warranty; Ford Motor Company warrants to owners as follows: That for 24 months or for 24,000 miles (3 months or 4,000 miles on Cobra V-8 engine and related power train components), whichever comes first, free replacement, including related labor, will be made by Ford Dealers of any part with a defect in workmanship or material. Tires are not covered by the warranty; appropriate adjustments will be made by tire companies. Owners will remain responsible for normal maintenance services, routine replacement of parts, such as filters, spark plugs, ignition points, wiper blades, brake and clutch linings, and normal deterioration of soft trim and appearance items. The warranty referred to herein is applicable to products sold in the U.S.A. and in certain neighboring areas.

The illustrations and product information contained herein were current at the time this publication was approved for printing. However, in order to continue to offer the finest automotive products available, Ford Motor Company reserves the right to change specifications, designs, models or prices without notice and without liability for such changes.

Mustang was flying high! Almost 700,000 units had now been built, and there was to be little change in the "new" 1966 model. Accordingly, there was little of great surprise. Although the grill ornamentation was simplified, and the side trim stripe revised, perhaps the biggest "change" was in the gas cap which had a new emblem. Certainly the use of the five-dial instrument panel and the hood lip molding has been anticipated on the GT models.

Production continued high, and Mustang had its best production year ever with 607,568 units produced, about ten percent more than in 1965. Production of the one millionth Mustang was reached in March, less than 24 months after introduction of the car, and commemorated accordingly by the production of a "Limited Edition Mustang" which featured the Six cylinder basic models dressed up with special wire wheel covers, side Accent Stripe and rocker panel molding (trim molding omitted), center console, chromed air cleaner and special engine decal.

Introduction of carpeted cowl and padded quarter panels and a bench seat option late in 1965 now reflected their installation: 63A Fastback 2+2; Standard Interior - 63B Fastback 2+2; Deluxe Interior - 76A Convertible; Standard Interior - 76B Convertible; Deluxe Interior - 65A Hardtop; Standard Interior - 65B Hardtop; Deluxe Interior.

Also, 76C Convertible, Bench Seat Option - 65C Hardtop, Bench Seat Option.

By 1966, the price of a Mustang Hardtop, delivered in Los Angeles, with small V-8, automatic transmission, power steering and radio, had reached over $3000.

1966 MUSTANG PRICES

MUSTANG MODELS	IBM Code	Body Code	
2-Door Hardtop	07	65A	$2,416.18(2)
Convertible	08	76A	2,652.86(2)
2 + 2 Fastback	09	63A	2,607.07(2)

8-Cylinder 289 CID 2-V Engine 200 HP—Extra Charge over 200 CID 1-V 120 HP 6-Cylinder	105.63

REGULAR PRODUCTION OPTIONS

ENGINES	
Extra Charge over 200 HP 289 CID Challenger V-8: 225 HP 289 CID 4-V Challenger Special V-8	52.85
271 HP Hi-Performance 289 CID 4-V Cobra V-8 (Includes Special Handling Package and 6.95 x 14 Dual Red Band Nylon Tires)	
With GT Equipment Group	276.34
Without GT Equipment Group	327.92
TRANSMISSIONS	
Cruise-O-Matic - 6-Cylinder Engine	175.80
Cruise-O-Matic - 8-Cylinder - 200 and 225 HP Engines	185.39
Cruise-O-Matic - 8-Cylinder 271 HP High Performance Engine	216.27
Four-Speed Manual - 6-Cylinder	113.45
Four-Speed Manual - 8-Cylinder	184.02
POWER ASSISTS	
Power Brakes	42.29
Power Steering	84.47
Power Top, Convertible	52.95
PERFORMANCE EQUIPMENT	
Battery - Heavy Duty-55 Amp.	7.44
Disc Brakes - Front - 8 Cylinder (N/A with Power Brakes)	56.77
GT Equipment Group - Available with 225 and 271 HP V-8 Engines Only (Includes Dual Exhaust System, Fog Lamps, Grille Bar, Special Ornamentation, Disc Brakes, Special Handling Package Components, GT Stripe—Less Rocker Panel Moulding	152.20
Limited Slip Differential	41.60
Rally-Pack - Clock/Tachometer	69.30
Special Handling Package - 200 and 225 HP V-8 Engines - includes increased rate front and rear springs, larger front and rear shock absorbers, 22 to 1 overall steering ratio, and larger diameter front stabilizer bar	30.64
Wheels, Styled Steel - 14" - 8-Cylinder Models only	93.84

All regular Mustang production options are available with the High Performance Engine except the following: Air Conditioning, 3-Speed Manual Transmission, Power Steering, US Royal tires. Regular Production Options available with the GT Equipment Group except the following: Power Brakes, Accent Stripe, and options not available when ordered with the High Performance Engine. Full width seat with center arm rest is not available with Interior Decor Group, Model 63A or Console options.

SAFETY EQUIPMENT	
Electric Windshield Wipers, 2-Speed	12.95
Glass, Tinted with Banded Windshield	30.25
Glass, Tinted, Windshield only	21.09
Seat Belts - Deluxe, Front and Rear - Front Retractors and Warning Light	14.53
Visibility Group - Includes Remote Control Mirror, Day/Nite Mirror, and 2-Speed Electric Wipers	29.81
COMFORT—CONVENIENCE EQUIPMENT	
Air Conditioner - Ford (Tinted Glass Recommended)	310.90
AM Radio - Stereosonic Tape System (Radio - Required)	128.49
Front Seat, Full Width/Arm Rest (65A and 76A)	24.42
Luggage Rack - Rear Deck Lid (65A and 76A)	32.44
Radio and Antenna	57.51
APPEARANCE EQUIPMENT	
Accent Stripe - Less Rear Quarter Ornamentation	$ 13.90
Console - Full Length	50.41
Console - For use with Air Cond.	31.52
Deluxe Steering Wheel - Simulated Wood Grain	31.52
Interior Decor Group - Includes Special Interior Trim, Deluxe Wood Grain Steering Wheel, R/W Door Courtesy Lights, and Pistol Grip Door Handle	94.13
Vinyl Roof - 65A	74.36
Wire Wheel Covers	58.24
Wheel Covers - Knock-Off Hubs	19.48
SPECIAL EQUIPMENT	
Closed Crankcase Emission System - Available only with Exh. ECS except with 271 HP Engine	5.19
Exhaust Emission Control System - N/A with 271 HP Engine	45.45
DELETE OPTIONS	
MagicAire Heater	(31.52)
OPTIONAL TIRE PRICES	
The following models have (5) 6.95 x 14 4-p.r. BSW Rayon tires as standard equipment: All models except those equipped with the 289 CID High Performance Engine	
Extra Charge for:	
(5) 6.95 x 14 4-p.r. WSW	33.31
(5) 6.95 x 14 4-p.r. BSW, Nylon	15.67
(5) 6.95 x 14 4-p.r. WSW, Nylon	48.89
(5) 6.95 x 14 4-p.r. Dual Red Band Nylon	48.97
The following models have (5) 6:95 x 14 4 p.r. Dual Red Band Nylon tires as standard equipment: All models with the 289 CID High Performance Engine	
No extra charge for the substitution of: (5) 6.96 x 14 4-p.r. Black or White - sidewall Nylon tires.	

1966 Mustang GT Convertible

Mrs. Jo Miller, Oceanside, California

1966 Mustang GT Hardtop

1966 Mustang GT Fastback 2+2

Mr. Ray Miller, Oceanside, California

1966 Mustang Hardtop *Mrs. Betty Hinsey, Crown Valley, California*

Mr. Fred Meyers, La Mesa, California

1966 Mustang Hardtop *Mr. Donald Nelson, Carlsbad, California*

The Convertible's durable 5-ply Vinyl top is available in either black or white. It is manually folded although an optional Power Top is available at extra cost. Easy-action side clamps (manual top only) secure the folded top frame and matching top "boot" is provided which snaps into place and protects the folded top. Foam latex cut-outs are provided to line the rear corners of the boot and thus add a more rounded shape there and also to protect the boot from being pierced by the exposed roof irons.

The Convertible Tonneau Cover (not shown), an Option whose use is limited to that model, provided a protection for the interior when top was lowered by snap-fastening a cover over the passenger compartment. A zipper, running lengthwise, allowed either half to be opened.

The 1966 grill ornament has no "arms" extending from the corral. New 1966 grill emphasizes horizontal lines and replaces earlier hexagonal pattern.

F—O—R—D letters continue on the hood lip.

Although fog lights themselves are identical, a different grill emblem assembly is used with the 1966 GT Models. Similar to the 1965 style (page 96), it differs in not having vertical struts above and below the corral.

Original headlamp bulbs bear the Fomoco name at their center.

The use of amber lenses on the standard turn-signal and parking light is continued.

The corners of the 1966 hood, like the identical 1965, are folded under and lack the distinctive "skirt" found on the 1964½ models (page 33).

The decorative "gills" at the sides of the radiator grill housing are non-functional. The headlamp bezel is a casting which nicely extends the fender lines.

GT Option adds fog lights at the sides of the grill.

Parallel-acting dual windshild wipers are standard. Available at extra cost is a two-speed electric wiper and windshield washer.

One of Mustang's options calls for a tinted windshield; another extends this to tinted glass in *all* windows.

The hood lip molding, first used on the GT models only, when they appeared late in the 1965 model year, is now standard on all 1966 models.

14" wheels are standard on all models for 1966, and several choices of dress-up wheels and covers are offered. See page 305 and following.

Radio antenna, furnished with that accessory, is mounted on the right front fender.

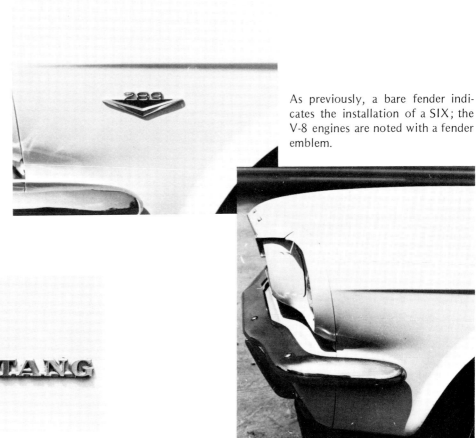

As previously, a bare fender indicates the installation of a SIX; the V-8 engines are noted with a fender emblem.

On standard models, the Mustang name and emblem continue to appear on front fenders. Fastback has additional "2+2" as in 1965 (page 53), but the special GT emblem and name appears on those models (top photo).

Rocker panel moldings are an optional accessory, also available with the Accent Paint Stripe option in which the side air scoop ornament is omitted.

The GT Option also omits the side air scoop ornament, but adds a decorative side stripe.

The same windshield glass is used on all body styles from 1964½ through 1967. The trim, however, differs between the closed cars and the Convertible which has bright-metal corner post moldings.

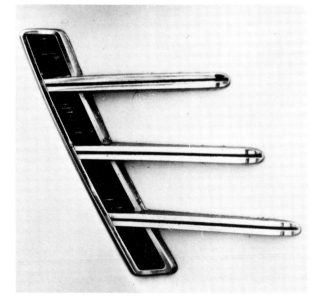

The 1966 side air scoop ornament emphasizes thrust by extended horizontal struts.

A "cap" at the back of the rear fender extends over the wrap-around bumper, visually integrating the area.

The pushbutton door handles are unchanged.

The bright-metal framed curved side window glass is a styling feature of the Mustang.

The rear window of the Hardtop is curved, and the body metal surrounding it is recessed for effect.

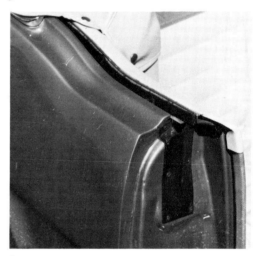

Quarter windows on the Hardtop and the Convertible can be lowered to a fully concealed position.

The standard rear end treatment for 1966 finds bumper guards on the lower valance panel. When the GT Option appears, these guards are replaced by the special exhaust tips (above).

The large side-to-side rear window of the Hardtop gives excellent rearward visibility. Convertible model has a zippered plastic rear window, and the Fastback 2+2 features a 10 square foot "skylight" rear window.

Initially conceived as three separate lights for 1966, the idea was abandoned and the earlier style continued.

No change occurs in the rear deck keylock latches.

Back-up lights are standard on all models for 1966.

The rear lower valance panel contains mounting holes for back-up lights and bumper guards. The GT valance panel differs.

New gas caps appeared for 1966, with a special GT cap used with that option alone.

Mustang's Platform Construction places special emphasis on jacking points, and a label, placed inside the rear deck lid (right) illustrates the required lifting points.

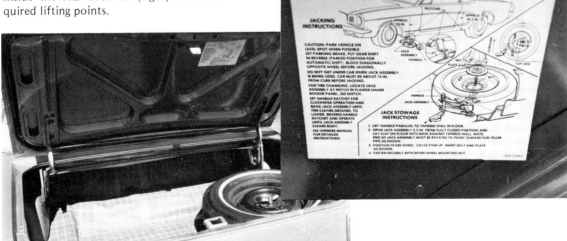

A scissors jack, with a special reversible-socket handle is standard equipment again in 1966.

STANDARD INTERIOR

Two interiors are available in 1966, the standard, and the "Luxury Interior" seen on the following pages. Standard interiors are available in five attractive all-vinyl combinations featuring a distinctive "woven" panel insert.

Inside door panels feature horizontal lined pattern rather than the vertical lines of the 1965 style (page 55).

Standard soft-padded arm rests are again installed on chromed brackets.

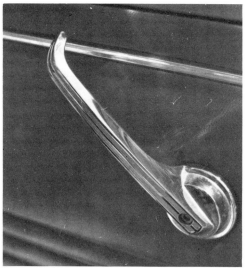

Window risers and door handles used with the standard interior are unchanged from the later 1965 style.

For the last year, the black background appears in the Ford oval on the door sill plates.

The 1966 Mustang standard bucket seats are upholstered in the same pattern as those in 1965. However, the pleated inserts are made of special "woven" texture vinyl (see below), and the seat backs are no longer heat-embossed with the stripe pattern found on the 1965 seats (page 61).

A new seat back rest appears in 1966 (see page 58).

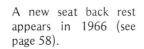

The fold-down rear seat of the Fastback 2+2 has simple pleated pattern.

A new Fastback 2+2 seat back latch, omitting the fixed bumper, appeared on early 1966 models. Later, a return was made to the earlier style (page 58).

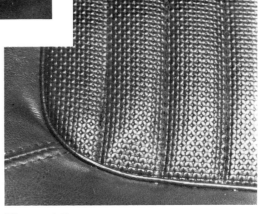

The specially textured "woven" vinyl inserts of 1966 differ from the smoothly textured 1965 style.

LUXURY INTERIOR

The Interior Decor Group Option features several distinctive items. Embossed seat inserts, door panels with pistol grip door handles, built-in arm rests, and courtesy lights, deluxe steering wheel and walnut panel trims are included.

The commonly used expression "Pony Interior" derives from the special seat inserts used with this option.

Walnut dress-up trim appliques are used on the Instrument Panel and the Glove Box door.

Special moulded door insert panels are featured.

Walnut-trimmed pistol grips replace the standard door handles.

The moulded door panels feature arm rests with a recessed door-pull.

Standard window riser handles are unchanged.

Safety-courtesy lights are built into the bottom of the doors and a red light shines rearward when door is opened.

This special embossed vinyl panel with its metal-trimmed center appears on the front seat backs of all models and the rear seats of the Hardtop and the Convertibles.

Rear seat of Hardtop with optional Interior Decor Group (rear seat belts are standard for 1966 on all models).

The rear quarter inside panel of the standard models is made of textured metal; on the Luxury cars, it is padded and a corner cap (upper left) is used.

The Interior Decor Group Option is easily spotted by its use of embossed inserts on the seat backs of both Hardtops and Convertibles, and on the front seat backs (only) of the Fastback 2+2.

Mustang's standard rear view mirror (top left) is suspended from an attractively-styled support arm which also serves to anchor the standard dual sun visors.

Separate switches are employed to operate the Power Top and the Fog Lights of the GT-equipped Convertibles.

At the hub of the Deluxe Steering Wheel appears a removable cap which is similar in appearance to the hub of the standard steering wheel.

The woodlike Deluxe Steering Wheel, a part of the Interior Decor Group option is also available separately. The holes in its spokes are pierced, not painted, and horn-blowing buttons are placed at the ends of the spokes (right). The wheel is slightly smaller in diameter than the standard wheel, measuring just over 15½ inches.

Okay, you can stop asking,
"Why doesn't Mustang bolt Cruise-O-Matic
behind the 271 solid-lifter V-8"?

For 1966, Ford offered their 3-speed Cruise-O-Matic automatic transmission as an option with the big 271 hp High Performance engine which previously had only been available with the manual 4-speed transmission.

The three-armed center section of the standard steering wheel is one piece, unlike the Deluxe Wheel which has a removable center cap. Unlike the Deluxe Wheel which features pierced holes in its spokes, these are painted depressions.

The standard steering wheel has a solid color plastic 16" diameter rim with a three-spoked hub. Its five inch "dish" matches that of the Deluxe wheel, but its spokes have only three "holes" in place of the four found on each Deluxe spoke. Available colors include Blue, Red, Aqua, Parchment, and Black.

The hub of the standard wheel bears the same decoration as appears on the Deluxe steering wheel (previous page).

The 1966 Instrument panel pad is similar to the 1965 style but at the center it curves downward around the radio.

An Option in 1965, four-way emergency flashers became standard equipment for 1966 and are operated by a switch in the glove compartment.

The Mustang insignia is continued on the glove box door. Walnut veneer indicates the presence of the Interior Decor Group option.

The round sweep-indicator 140 mph speedometer first appeared in late 1965 on the GT models and became standard for 1966.

An ammeter and an oil pressure gauge (below left) are standard for 1966 replacing the warning lights used in 1965. The rectangular windows in these views are turn signal light indicators.

A MUSTANG THAT ISN'T A "MUSTANG"

1966 T-5 Fastback 2+2

*Mr. Bob Ogle,
San Diego, California*

Not generally realized is the fact that Mustangs have always been available for export, and are extremely popular in certain countries. One such is Germany, where, coincidentally, the rights to the name "Mustang" are owned by someone other than Ford. Accordingly, every Mustang completed for export to that country is identified not by the common name, but rather as a "T-5" (which is the <u>original</u> designation of the Mustang project), and all use of the word eliminated. As late as the Fall of 1977, the T-5 designation was still being used in this connection.

M–U–S–T–A–N–G name on front fenders is replaced with T-5 nameplate.

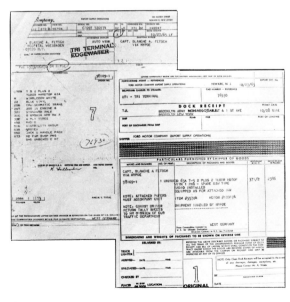

On October 27, 1965, this T-5 2+2 was forwarded by Ford Motor Company's Export Supply Operations to Weisbaden, Germany.

T-5 horn ring resembles domestic part (page 119), but lacks the Mustang name.

TYPICAL 1965/66 ACCESSORIES

On this and the following pages, we show accessories which are typical of those available at the time. Unless otherwise noted, these are all 1964½-1966 options, and available as Dealer-installed items as well as at the Dealer's Parts Departments.

The Rally-Pac, a popular Option, bolts to the steering column, adding a tachometer and a clock.

The word "Rally-Pac" appears on the web of the 1964½ units and also on those sold as Service Parts (after-market) by Ford's Dealers through 1966.

Tachometers are connected in <u>series</u> with the coil, and a failure of the instrument opens the ignition circuit.

A 6000 rpm tachometer is used with all engines except the High Performance V-8.

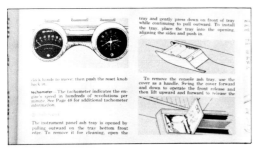

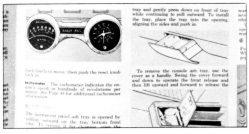

Owner's Manual for 1964½ (bottom) and 1965 (top) show elimination of Rally-Pac name.

The 1965 factory installation eliminates the name Rally-Pac from the web, but instruments are the same.

The 8000 rpm instrument is supplied with the High Performance engine which is designed to operate well above 6000 rpm.

The web is narrowed and unmarked.

The clock face matches tachometer.

After early 1966, the factory-installed Rally-Pac has sweep-indicator tachometer and matching clock.

Again an 8000 rpm tachometer is available for use with the High Performance engine.

A former bright-metal bezel is omitted.

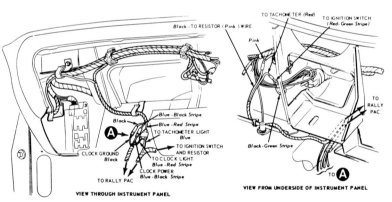

Rally Pac Wiring Connections

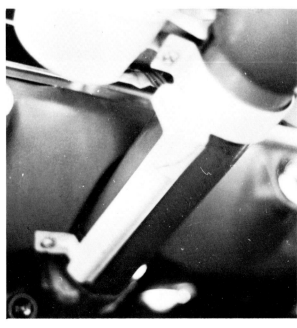

A channel is furnished with the 1966 Rally-Pac which conceals its wires.

A belt-driven compressor, placed under the hood, is part of the installation.

The gray-faced air conditioner was factory-installed in 1965 and also sold as an after-market Service Accessory through 1966.

Air-conditioners are bolt-on, rather than behind-the-dash units, and their controls are on the front face.

Four adjustable vanes allow directed air circulation.

For 1966, the adjustable vanes are simplified and lose their inner concentric circle.

The 1966 factory-installed air conditioner has a black face, but is generally interchangable with the earlier style.

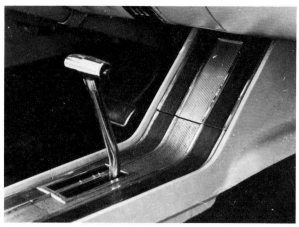

Ford's "Unique Console" is a popular dress-up option. Full-length, it serves to divide the front compartment, and is cut-out for transmission shift lever.

An ash tray is built into the rear of the console as is an auxiliary courtesy light.

When installed with an air conditioning unit, a shorter-length console (which can be made from the longer unit) is necessary. A trim plate (above) then closes the front end of the console beneath the air conditioner.

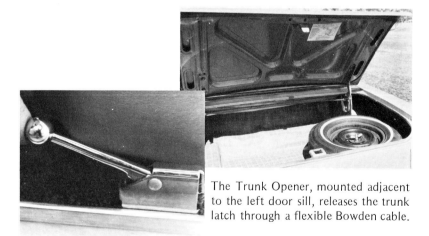

The Trunk Opener, mounted adjacent to the left door sill, releases the trunk latch through a flexible Bowden cable.

An instrument-panel mounted clock is available as an alternate to the Rally-Pac.

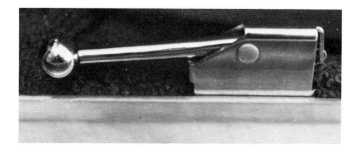

125

TYPICAL 1965/66 ACCESSORIES

The 1965 Day-Night rear view mirror has a rocker-type adjustment.

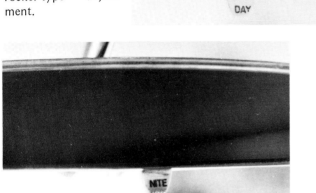

The 1966 Day-Night mirror has a turn-screw adjustment.

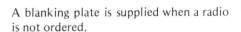

A blanking plate is supplied when a radio is not ordered.

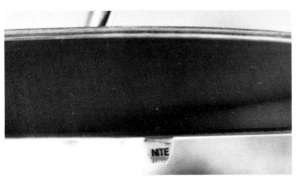

A Push-button AM Radio is one option.

Introduced in 1966, the AM/FM radio is a rare option. The Mustang unit can be distinguished by the word F—O—R—D on its slide bar.

Another 1966 Option is the stereo AM-Tape player. Furnished complete with in-door speakers (although the panel-mounted speaker is omitted), the unit is larger and its control knobs are located differently; an external faceplate is included to conceal standard holes.

One Option is a universal outside rear view mirror.

A remote-adjusting Outside Rear View Mirror is also available. Another Option is a matching, but non-remote, right side mirror.

An after-market accessory, these chrome trim plates dress up the "gills" on either side of the radiator grill.

Now—just in time for Christmas—
only at your Ford Dealer's!

MIDGET MUSTANG

Specially priced at only
$12.95
While they last!

Best year yet to go Ford

MUSTANG!
MUSTANG!
MUSTANG!

The Accent Paint Stripe Option deletes the standard side air scoop ornament, and is generally furnished with a dress-up Rocker Panel Molding, another Option.

A special introductory promotional item, the all-metal pedal-operated Midget Mustang was offered in November of 1964 at a special low $12.95 price.

Introduced in 1965, the optional Bench Front seat formed the basis for special Body Style Codes (page 101). Although expanding seating capacity, the Bench Seat, despite a pull-down arm rest, was never a popular option.

A "Negative Option" deletion of a standard Heater/Defroster substitutes a blanking plate in the firewall and credited the purchaser for the omitted heater.

Back-lighted grill ornaments were non-Ford initially, but later, in 1966, and 1967 (above right), Ford made the part available at its Parts Counters.

Ford dress-up license plate frames add to the appearance of the car.

Ford Tissue Dispensers are available to suspend under the instrument panel.

A rare accessory, this Dealer-installed Folding Sun Roof is a highly desirable addition to the Hardtop or the Fastback 2+2.

Bright stainless-steel door sill accessory moldings cover exposed portion of the sill adjacent to the standard aluminum scuff plates.

"Pony" hood ornament is after-market accessory.

"Pony" bumperettes are an after-market accessory.

Vinyl Roof Covering for the Hardtop, in Black or White, is a factory Option.

The under-hood Trouble Light is also used as a lamp for the luggage compartment.

The deck-mounted Luggage Rack is an option limited by its size to the Hardtop and Convertible.

The Trailer Hitch is another Dealer-installed Option.

A Dealer-installed accessory for 1966, the Collapsible Spare Tire became a factory Option in 1967.

1965/66 ACCESSORIES

Special "Mustang Sun Glasses" were an after-market accessory.

Late in 1964, the editors of Automobile Quarterly, prominent automotive magazine, commissioned Carrozzeria Bertone of Turin to design and build a special-bodied Mustang to be shown at the 1965 New York International Automobile Show. A conventional Fastback 2+2 was shipped to Turin to be rebodied in the style of a traditional Italian GT. The car was lowered on special 14" wheels, frontal area reduced and lowered (the radiator height had also to be reduced), and larger glass areas fitted. The roof is of brushed stainless steel and is supported by a built-in roll bar. After the showing in New York, where it won "best of show", the car was again shipped overseas to be shown in England, Italy, France, and Germany. Through an incredible paperwork blunder this lovely car was "misplaced" and can not now be located.

1965 Mustang GT Convertible with Dealer-installed removable Hardtop.

A New York City Custom Coachbuilder re-bodied this 1965 Mustang in an appeal to suburban market but had limited success.

130

The vinyl Tonneau Cover is a factory Option for the Convertible, and is offered in White or Black.

. Jim Panthana, Columbus, Ohio

Reminiscent of the early Thunderbirds, this attractive removable Hardtop was Dealer-furnished and converted the Convertible into a snug Hardtop.

There were many, many more Options. Some of the many available in 1965 include:

- *door edge guards*
- *spotlight*
- *vanity mirror*
- *fire extinguisher*
- *compass*
- *rear seat speaker*
- *windshield washers*
- *glove box lock*
- *disc brakes*
- *power steering & brakes*
- *floor mats*
- *parking brake warning light*
- *back-up lights (1965 only; standard in 1966)*
- *"studio sonic" reverberator sound system*
- *"lake pipes" (side exhaust kits) and*
- *"Cobra High Performance kits" which increased the output of the 289 engine line*

ENGINES

Mustang was introduced as an all-purpose car, and one such purpose was to provide an economical, sturdy, family-type car. Dealers were exhorted in factory selling aids to "Sell the SIX", and an excellent job was done in this connection, but Buyers ignored the pressure. Only about 30% of the cars were equipped with this engine.

The 1964½ SIX, Mustang's standard engine for the time, was a 170 cubic inch displacement, single-barrel carburetor equipped, single exhaust, power plant rated at 101 horsepower. All three transmission options (3-speed, 4-speed, and Automatic) were offered with this engine.

All 1964½ engines were equipped with DC generators in the charging circuit. The generator drive pulley on the High Performance engine was larger to compensate for that engine's higher operating speed.

Three V-8 extra cost Options were offered. The smallest was the 260 cid, two barrel carburetor, single exhaust engine rated at 164 horsepower. With a compression ration of 8.7:1, like the SIX, it used regular fuel and was a popular option. Only the 3-speed and automatic transmissions were offered.

In addition, the 289 engine (following pages) was offered with a four barrel carburetor, single exhaust, and a 9.0:1 compression ratio rated at 210 HP. Finally, the High Performance 289, four barrel carburetor (manual choke) and dual exhaust, offered a rated 271 horsepower and a mammoth 10.0:1 compression ratio, offered a rated Two-Hundred-and-Seventy-One Horsepower!

The 210 HP engine was offered with either 4-speed or Automatic, but only the 4-speed was offered with the High Performance engine.

By early fall, the new 1965 Mustang's power plants were gaining in size and strength. A new SIX offered almost twenty percent more horsepower; the 260 cid V-8 was dropped, and Ford's ubiquitous 289 cid V-8 appeared in two _new_ versions plus the High Performance Screamer.

Now rated at 120 horsepower, the SIX has a higher compression ratio (9.2:1), but only a single-barrel carburetor.

Alternators replaced the DC generators on all 1965 engines.

Distributor has vacuum-operated Advance.

Identification tags are secured to each engine.

Optional Challenger 289 V-8 is 2-barrel carburetor version rated at 200 horsepower, has 9.3:1 compression ratio. "Bigger" engine, 4-barrel carburetor-equipped, 10.0:1 compression Challenger Special (right) is rated at 225 HP, required Premium fuel.

ENGINES

1966 Challenger Special 289 V-8 equipped with optional valve covers and high-rise intake manifold.

Starting with the GT units of late 1965, an oil pressure sensing unit is installed adjacent to the oil filter. Fuel pump is unchanged.

The chromed oil filler cap is an option. Hose leading to carburetor is part of valve cover Emission Control System introduced in 1964.

Radiator coolant temperature is affected by thermostat placed in neck of intake manifold.

Letters C6AE in head casting indicates the 4-V premium fuel 225 HP Challenger Special engine.

Optional Cobra dress up valve covers were offered by Ford as early as February of 1964. Identical to those used on the Shelby-American Cobras and GT 350, they are (from top) "no hole" covers used on non-emission reduction or intake manifold Emission Reduction System 289 engines (prior to 1964), 289 engines with rocker arm cover ERS, late 1966 (and present day replacement) style with solid lettering, and the 1967 style offered by Shelby-American after Cobra name was sold to Ford.

Initially the rocker arms in the valve train of the 289 engines were cast with a small boss to bear against the valve stem, and the push rods worked in oval slots in the heads.

Rocker arm studs are pressed into the heads.

Late in 1967, a change was made in the rocker arm (left) and "rails" added.

After 1968 the rocker arm straddled the valve stem, and simple round holes for the push rods were placed in the heads.

The face of the 289 pistons is counter-bored to clear valves, and additionally to lower compression on other than High Performance engines.

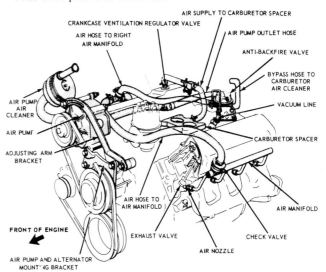

With some few exceptions, cars sold in California after Jan. 1, 1966, were equipped with the Thermactor System which is a means by which fresh air, injected under pressure at the exhaust valves, burns exhaust gases in the manifold.

Noting that improved "breathing" is a major area of adding horsepower to an engine, Ford, in 1966, offered among their other High Performance Accessories, intake and exhaust manifolds designed to accomplish this purpose, claiming in their catalog a 25% increase in horsepower for the 200 HP engine achieved with these and a centrifugal-advance Distributor (page 139).

Two-barrel carburetor intake manifold, standard for 1966 289 cid Challenger 200 horsepower engine.

Ford accessory Performance Product is an aluminum high rise intake manifold for use with 289 cid engines.

Four-barrel carburetor intake manifold, standard for 1966 289 cid premium fuel Challenger Special 225 horsepower engine.

Stock 1965 289 cid engine exhaust manifold.

289 cid High Performance cast iron exhaust manifold (also sold as bolt-on accessory for 200 and 225 horsepower Challenger V-8's).

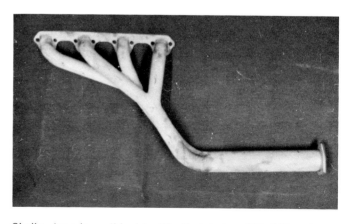

Shelby-American "double Wye" tubular GT 350 exhaust header.

The installation of the High Performance Engine is indicated by the letter "K" in the Vehicle Identification Number stamped under the hood. All GT 350 units thus have such a number under their Shelby-American Serial Number Plate.

289 cid High Performance 271 horsepower engine features heavy-duty crankshaft, rods, and caps, special camshaft, solid lifters, high compression heads, dual point ignition, and other performance items.

The High Performance Flag is a plate inserted behind the standard 289 fender badge. Although the engine can be replicated, and the "flag" added, *original* High Performance cars can be detected by their serial numbers.

High Performance Engine Owner's Manual.

Pistons have cast-in "eyebrows" for valve clearence. Lower compression 2V version (right) has additional center depression, and HP units (not shown) also have two raised pads to close valves in case of high speed spring "float".

Intake valves larger than exhaust.

The rocker arm studs are threaded into the heads of the High Performance engine, not pressed in as in the others.

ENGINES

The dual-point High Performance Distributor, available also as a bolt-on accessory for other 289 engines, has a mechanical Advance rather than the conventional vacuum-operated unit. (Centrifugal weights advance the spark as engine speed increases). Dual contacts increase the dwell angle from about 27 to about 34 degrees giving the coil a longer period in which to saturate. This added time improves the ignition efficiency by providing a "hotter" spark and is especially important at higher rpm. Heavier springs also minimize contact point "bounce".

All High Performance engines use a flat chromed air cleaner. However, the 1965 (left) cover is shaped differently than the 1966 style at the right.

Other Ford accessories include kits for the use of three 2-V carburetors or two 4-V units and are complete including the manifold, carburetors, linkages, and a special oval air cleaner. This air cleaner was sold, by Shelby-American as indicated by the COBRA name. After 1967, Shelby continued to offer a similar kit with the name SHELBY thereon as Ford took over Cobra's name.

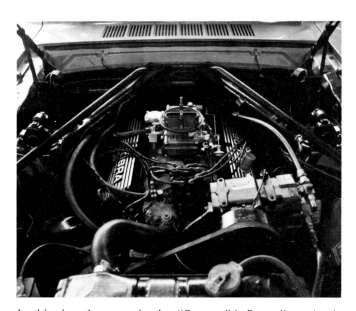

In this view the strengthening "Convertible Braces", used only in that model, can be seen reinforcing the front section.

ENGINE REMOVAL

The engine removal procedures are for the engine only without the transmission attached.

REMOVAL

1. Drain the cooling system and the crankcase. Remove the oil filter.

2. Remove the hood. Disconnect the battery ground cable at the cylinder block.

3. Disconnect the automatic choke heat chamber air inlet hose at the inlet tube near the right valve rocker arm cover. **Do not remove the air inlet hose at the air cleaner.** Remove the air cleaner and intake duct assembly.

4. Disconnect the radiator upper hose at the coolant outlet housing and the radiator lower hose at the water pump.

On a car with an automatic transmission, disconnect the transmission oil cooler lines at the radiator.

5. Remove the radiator. Remove the fan, spacer, belt, and pulley.

6. Disconnect the wires at the alternator. Loosen the alternator adjusting bolts to allow the alternator to swing down and out of the way.

7. Disconnect the oil pressure sending unit wire at the sending unit, and the flexible fuel line at the fuel tank line. Plug the fuel tank line.

8. Disconnect the accelerator rod at the bellcrank.

On a car with an automatic transmission, disconnect the throttle valve vacuum line at the intake manifold. Disconnect the manul shift rod at the bellcrank and remove the retracting spring. Disconnect the transmission filler tube bracket at the cylinder block.

On a car with an air conditioner, isolate and remove the compressor as outlined in Group 16.

On a car with power steering and air conditioning, remove the speedup control assembly from the bellcrank assembly.

On a car with power steering, disconnect the power sterring pump bracket from the cylinder head. Remove the drive belt. Wire the power steering pump out of the way and in a position that will prevent the oil from draining out. Disconnect the brake vacuum line at the intake manifold.

9. Remove the heater hose from the automatic choke housing. Disconnect the heater hoses at the water pump and intake manifold. Disconnect the water temperature sending unit wire at the sending unit.

10. Remove the flywheel or converter housing to engine upper bolts.

11. Disconnect the primary wire at the ignition coil and position the wire out of the way.

12. Raise the front of the car. Disconnect the starter cable at the starter. Remove the starter and dust seal.

13. Disconnect the muffler inlet pipes from the exhaust manifolds. Disconnect the engine support insulators at the brackets on the frame underbody.

On a car with a manual-shift transmission, remove the remaining flywheel housing to engine bolts.

On a car with an automatic transmission, remove the converter housing inspection cover. Disconnect the flywheel from the converter. Secure the converter assembly in the housing. Remove the remaining converter housing to engine bolts.

14. Lower the car, then support the transmission. Install the engine left lifting bracket at the front of the left cylinder head, and install the engine right lifting bracket at the rear of the right cylinder head, then attach the engine lifting sling (Fig. 58).

15. Remove the air cleaner duct stud from the exhaust manifold. Remove the battery.

16. Raise the engine slightly and carefully pull it from the transmission. Carefully lift the engine out of the engine compartment so that the rear cover plate is not bent or other components damaged. Install the engine on a work stand.

TRANSMISSIONS

A three-speed manual transmission is standard with all engines except the High Performance model. Two units are used, the one with the V-8 engine synchronized in all forward gears; that with the SIX in 2nd and direct only.

The floor-mounted manul shift lever is given a finished appearance with a flexible rubber boot and chromed retainer (also used with 4-speed).

Standard "H" shift pattern is employed and appears on the shift lever knob.

1966 Standard type brake pedal is identical with pedals used with Interior Decor Group but lack the bright-metal frame.

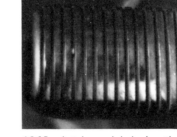

1965 clutch pedal lacks the indentations at the perimeter and design was discarded starting in late 1965.

Suspended pedals, a Mustang feature, include the accelerator.

The Warner T-10 4-speed transmission, optional with other engines is standard with the High Performance engine. Initially the only one available, it was later joined by the (optional) C-4 Cruise-O-Matic automatic transmission in late 1965.

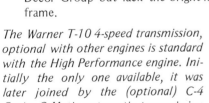

When the console is installed, it is fitted so that no change is necessary in the shift lever boot and retainer.

The 4-speed shift pattern appears on its shift lever knob. Reverse gear is locked out by a spring-loaded finger-pull just below the knob.

The Cruise-O-Matic 3-speed automatic transmission was initially available as an Option with all engines except the 271 horsepower High Performance (it was, however, added as a new option for 1966). The unit is a 3-speed lightweight gearbox in which gear ratios can be matched to road conditions almost like a manual shift, or, the unit will handle all gear-changing automatically.

The Cruise-O-Matic floor-mounted shift lever has a T-handle which incorporates a reverse gear lockout release button (left) and matching decorative button (right).

Standard P-R-N-D shift pattern is indicated on semi-circular floor plate (here and at left).

A fluid-filled torque converter is used at the input of the automatic transmission, and is coupled to the crankshaft.

Foot pedals furnished with Interior Decor Group have bright-metal trim; standard pedal (top) is plain.

EXHAUST SYSTEMS

The single exhaust pipe continues to the transversely-mounted muffler.

Two exhaust pipes of a V-8 converge into a single tube leading to the standard transverse-mounted muffler.

The standard exhaust system (including the smaller V-8 engines), is silenced by a transversely-mounted muffler placed in an upright position behind the rear axle and ahead of the fuel tank.

An outlet pipe extends from the muffler back, under the fuel tank, and exhausts sharply downward ahead of the rear lower valance panel.

A single-pipe exhaust system is standard, but a dual-exhaust system (standard on the High Performance engine) is an Option for the other V-8 engines.

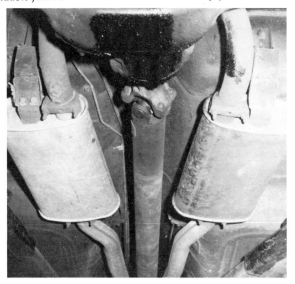

Larger diameter pipes (for lower restriction) are used on dual-exhaust systems which are essentially two separate single-exhausts joined at the front with this cross-pipe.

The transverse-mounted muffler is omitted in the dual-exhaust system.

Two individual oval mufflers are used in the dual-exhaust system with added resonators in each tail pipe.

On the GT Option, the exhaust tips protrude through the rear lower valance panel, others exit downward just ahead of the panel as seen on facing page.

Additional body stiffening is required for the Convertible which lacks the steel roof's rigidity. Reinforcing gussets and a distinctive "Convertible Plate" are used on that model (above) and do not appear on the Hardtop (right) or Fastback 2+2.

1967

Mustang '67

BODY TYPE

65A   2-door Hardtop
65B   2-door Hardtop; Luxury Trim
65C   2-door Hardtop; Bench Seat

63A   Fastback 2+2
63B   Fastback 2+2; Luxury Trim

76A   Convertible
76C   Convertible; Bench Seat
76D   Convertible; Luxury Trim

EXTERIOR COLOR CODE

Raven Black	*A*
Wimbleton White	*M*
Candyapple Red	*T*
Vintage Burgundy	*X*
Nightmist Blue	*K*
Brittany Blue	*Q*
Arcadian Blue	*F*
Clearwater Aqua	*W*
Frost Turquoise	*B*
Dark Moss Green	*Y*
Sauterne Gold	*Z*
Pebble Beige	*6*
Springtime Yellow	*8*
Burnt Amber	*V*
Lime Gold	*I*
Acapulco Blue	**D*

*Exclusively Mustang in 1967

1967 saw revisions to Mustang's grill and a new rear end treatment, and although wheelbase was unchanged, the car had a heavier look as a result of a widening of the bodies (70.9" in 1967 vs 68.2) and slightly increasing the overall height (51.6" against 51.1 earlier). The Fastback 2+2 featured a "full sloping roof" eliminating the distinctive break in the roof lines of the earlier model, and a number of new features were included in Ford's new standard "Lifeguard Design Safety" package including a dual hydraulic brake system, energy-absorbing steering wheel, padded impact areas, positive door locks (door lock buttons must be raised before doors can be opened), and others.

Among new Options offered in 1967 were the Tilt-Away Steering Wheel, the Overhead Map Light, Convenience Control Panel (which includes warning lights for parking brake, door ajar, low fuel, and seat belts), Power Front Disc Brakes, Automatic Speed Control, and a new Selectshift Cruise-O-Matic which gave the driver the choice of fully automatic shifting or manual shifting through the three forward gear ranges.

Under the hood, a new offering was the Thunderbird Special V-8, a 390 cubic inch giant boasting an unbelievable 320 horsepower or almost 20% more than last year's top choice 271 HP 289 cid High Performance engine! Testing this option in November of 1966, outstanding automotive publication Car & Driver noted . . . "Fastest of the current sporty-type cars from Detroit—including Camaro, Barracuda, Marlin, and Cougar".

1967 Mustang Specifications

Color and Upholstery Selections: Pick your favorite color from 16 brilliant new Super Diamond Lustre Enamel single tones. Counting standard and optional choices, there are a total of 20 all-vinyl trims for the hardtop, 18 for 2+2, 16 for convertible. Your Ford Dealer will be happy to show you samples of new Mustang colors & upholsteries.

Engines (see chart for availability): **200-cu. in. Six—** 120 hp; 3.68" bore x 3.13" stroke; 9.2 to 1 comp. ratio; 7 main bearings; reg. fuel; single-barrel carb.; auto. choke; self-adj. valves with hydraulic lifters.

289-cu. in. Challenger V-8 — 200 hp; 4.00" bore x 2.87" stroke; 9.3 to 1 comp. ratio; reg. fuel; 2-barrel carb.; auto. choke; self-adj. valves with hydraulic lifters.

289-cu. in. Challenger Special V-8—225 hp; 4.00" bore x 2.87" stroke; 9.8 to 1 comp. ratio; 4-barrel carb.; prem. fuel. Other specifications same as Challenger V-8 above.

289-cu. in. Cobra V-8—271 hp; 4.00" x 2.87" stroke; 10.0 to 1 comp. ratio; prem. fuel; 4-barrel carb.; manual choke; solid valve lifters; dual exhaust.

390-cu. in. Thunderbird Special V-8—320 hp; 4.05" bore x 3.78" stroke; 10.5 to 1 comp. ratio; prem. fuel; 4-barrel carb.; auto. choke; self-adj. valves; oil cap'y, incl. filter, 5 qt.; dual exhaust.

Engine Features: 6000-mile (or 6-month) full-flow disposable-type oil filter; replaceable dry element air cleaner; 190° thermostat; 12-volt electrical system with 38-amp. alternator; 42-amp. alternator on High Performance V-8; 54-plate, 45 amp-hr battery; weatherproof ignition; positive-engagement starter; fully aluminized muffler and tailpipe. All engines are electronically mass-balanced for long-lived smoothness.

13 Mustang Power Teams

Engines	Transmissions
200-Cu. In. Six*	S*, C
289-Cu. In. Challenger V-8	S*, C, 4
289-Cu. In. Challenger Special V-8	S*, C, 4
289-Cu. In. Cobra V-8	4, C
390-Cu. In. Thunderbird Special V-8	S, C, 4

*Standard equipment; all others optional

Transmission Key:
S — Synchro-Smooth Drive (fully synchronized 3-speed manual)
C — Cruise-O-Matic Drive   4 — 4-Speed Manual

Manual Transmissions (see chart for availability): **Synchro-Smooth Drive.** Synchronized manual shifting in all three forward gears; clash-free downshifting to low while under way. Floor-mounted stick, standard "H" pattern.

4-Speed Manual. Sports-type close-ratio transmission, synchronized in all forward gears; floor-mounted stick.

SelectShift Cruise-O-Matic Drive: Lets you drive fully automatic or shift manually through the gears. Three forward speeds, one reverse. Effective engine braking in low gear (1) for better control on grades and hills. Quadrant sequence (P-R-N-D-2-1).

Rear Axle: Semi-floating hypoid rear axle; straddle-mounted drive pinion (V-8's). Permanently lubricated wheel bearings.

Front Suspension: Angle-Poised Ball-Joint type with coil springs mounted on upper arms. 36,000-mile (or 3-year) lube intervals. Strut-stabilized lower arms. Link-type, rubber-bushed ride stabilizer.

Rear Suspension: Longitudinal, 4-leaf springs with rubber-bushed front mounts, compression-type shackles at rear. Asymmetrical, variable-rate design with rear axle located forward of spring centers for anti-squat on takeoff. Diagonally mounted shock absorbers.

Steering: Recirculating ball-type steering gear provides easy handling. Permanently lubricated steering linkage joints. Overall steering ratio 25.4 to 1 (power steering 20.3 to 1). Turning diameter 38 ft.

Brakes: New dual hydraulic brake system with dual master cylinder, separate lines to front and rear brakes. Self-adjusting, self-energizing design. Composite drums grooved for extra cooling: 9" (Six), 10" (V-8's). Total lining areas: 131 sq. in. (Six), 154 sq. in. (V-8's).

Tires: Tubeless, blackwall with Tyrex rayon cord, 4-ply rating. Safety-type rims. Tire size—6.95 x 14.

Dimensions & Capacities: Length 183.6"; width 70.9"; height: hardtop 51.6", fastback 51.8", convertible 51.6"; wheelbase 108"; treads 58"; trunk luggage volume (cu. ft.): hardtop 9.2, convertible 7.7 (top down), fastback 5.1 (18.5 with optional rear seat folded down); fuel 17 gal.

Approximate Weights: Mustang Hardtop, 2695 lb. (Six), 2885 lb. (V-8); Mustang Fastback 2+2, 2725 lb. (Six), 2915 lb. (V-8); Mustang Convertible, 2855 lb. (Six), 3045 lb. (V-8).

1967 Mustang 65A Hardtop *Mr. Ed Edson, Las Vegas, Nevada*

1967 Mustang 76C Convertible *Mrs. Margaret Merlock, Oceanside, California*

1967 Mustang 63A Fastback 2+2 *Mr. John McMullen, Jr. Vista, California*

In this October 15, 1966 advertisement, Mustang's newest options (power front disc brakes and tilt-away steering wheel) are mentioned for what may be the first time.

1967 Mustang 65A Hardtop with Optional Vinyl Roof   *Ms. Lee Garver, Los Angeles County, California*

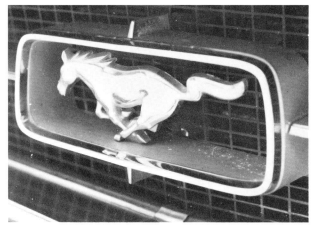

A new higher grill alters the appearance of the front end. Somewhat similar to the 1965 style, the grill ornament again has horizontal bars.

Short vertical accents add to the revised "corral" which is now wider at the bottom rather than at the top like the earlier style, page 50.

The lettered F—O—R—D is retained on the hood lip.

Gone are the "gills" of the earlier style (page 50) and the headlamps made to appear larger by an added bezel.

New standard parking-and-turn-signal lights with *clear* lenses are recessed further into the lower front valance panel, losing their former chromed bezel.

The standard hood has familiar "windsplit" crease down its length. Dual windshield wipers with washers are now standard.

The new grill ornament has added depth, and only its forward edges are chromed.

Revised grill detail includes a new hood latch mechanism replacing the earlier style (page 52).

Part of the optional "Exterior Decor Group" (which also includes wheel cut-out moldings, rear deck lid molding, and pop-open gas cap) a new "breather" hood has functional louvers with built-in turn-signal indicator lamps.

Optional rocker panel molding (standard on the 2+2) for 1967 is smooth, not ribbed as was the earlier style (page 110).

The adjustable outside rear view mirror became standard equipment starting in 1967.

Starting in 1967, the added "2+2" emblem (page 53) was no longer used on that model, and (except on GT) all body styles carried only a lettered M-U-S-T-A-N-G.

Dual die-cast non-functional intake grills are standard on the sides of all models for 1967.

Basic side emblem is that used with the SIX.

The optional V-8 engines are commemorated with their cubic inch displacement added to the side emblems; a similar emblem bears the "390" legend.

Vinyl roof covering in Black or Parchment, is an available Option for the Hardtop only.

The bright-metal trim at the base of the roof (above left) is a part of the Vinyl Roof option and does not appear as standard equipment.

Options include tinted glass all around or in the windshield only. The standard rear window of the 2+2 is tinted.

A new simplified 12-louver pattern appears on the Fastback 2+2 in place of the five-section assembly used previously (page 57).

Beneath the familiar outside door handle is a new keylock accommodating 1967's new "reversible keys" which can be inserted either way.

Flexible-backed day/night inside rear view mirrors are standard starting in 1967.

1967

The addition of an accessory rear deck lip molding (above) emphasizes width over the appearance of the standard rear end (below).

A new Option for 1967 is a glass folding rear window for the Convertible. Two panes of tempered safety glass are hinged with translucent silicone rubber and fold with the roof.

New rear bumper guards are painted body color (right), but have a rubber facing strip.

The use of Easy-Open safety catches for the folded non-Power Convertible top is continued.

New rear deck keylock accepts reversible key.

The embossed line at the rear curves upward inboard of the tail lights on a Fastback 2+2 and passes over the block letters of the Mustang name.

On the Convertible and Hardtop, the embossed line *drops* inboard of the tail lights.

A wired-on gas cap is standard, but a new option, the Exterior Decor Group, includes a pop-open gas cap.

Rear deck lid moldings are part of the optional Exterior Decor Group.

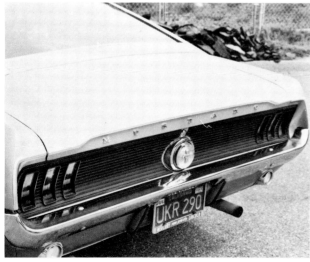

The Rear Deck Grill is a separate option available with the Exterior Decor Group. Made of aluminum it replaces the individual chromed tail light covers.

1967

Door locks have been redesigned and the inside lock buttons must be pulled up to unlock; inside handle will not over-ride.

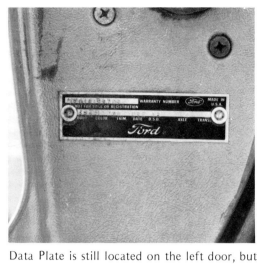

Vent window locking handles have new shape.

Data Plate is still located on the left door, but has been lowered and is now installed *below* the door latch.

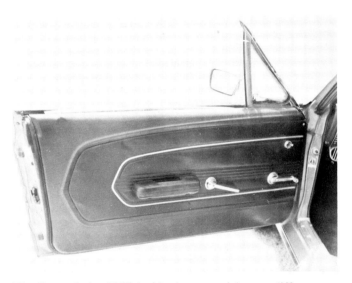

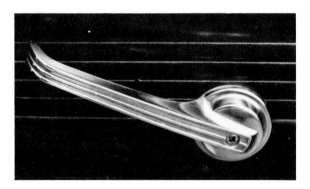

The lines of the 1967 inside door panel inserts differ somewhat from 1966 (page 114), but the standard interior's arm rest and handles are unchanged.

The inside door panels of the Interior Decor ("luxury") Option feature molded-in arm rests, behind-the-grill courtesy lights, and a brushed-aluminum dress up panel matching the instrument panel.

Standard inside door handle is rotated and Decor panel slipped over it.

A new rectangular Remote Rear View Mirror replaces the earlier round style (page 127).

Starting in 1967, blue paint is used on the door sill emblem plate in place of black.

Standard inside door panels do not have the brushed aluminum dress-up panels found on the "luxury" panels.

The Seat Belt Reminder Light is a new optional safety reminder. The light glows when ignition switch is turned on but goes out automatically after a few seconds.

The turn-signal lever, starting in 1967, has a lane-changing feature to enable brief activation prior to such a move without the need to complete a turn.

For 1967, Mustang offered all-vinyl upholstery available in seven color choices, featuring color-keyed carpeting. Again the optional Interior Decor Group added special trim and lighting features for an added "luxury" effect.

Starting in 1967, the optional Air Conditioner was placed behind the instrument panel and appropriate outlet vents provided (above). Those cars delivered without air conditioning lacked these features (right).

Mustang stressed "Built-In Safety" features for 1967. Part of this program were such items as the padding applied at the steering wheel hub, windshield pillars, and lower instrument panel.

A new Option for 1967 is the Tilt-Away Steering Wheel, adjustable to any of nine up-and-down positions, and which moves sideways out of the way when ignition is turned off.

An optional overhead console containing individual map lights is a part of the Interior Decor Group option and is supplied in Hardtop and Fastback 2+2 only.

Color-keyed to the interiors, the 1967 standard steering wheel is available in seven colors, Blue, Red, Aqua, Black, Parchment (the 1966 colors) plus Saddle and Ivy Gold.

The standard 4-Way Emergency Flasher switch is placed on the steering column.

A new Deep-Padded steering wheel hub adds to safety.

Over 100 separate Options were offered with the 1967 Mustang. Some like the Tilt-Away steering wheel and the Fingertip Speed Control (built in 1967 into the turn-signal lever) were of practical value, and persisted in subsequent models. Others, such as the Overhead Map Light and the Convenience Control Panel did not. Surprisingly, Mustang offered a citizen's band mobile radio in 1967; but it found only limited acceptance and was later discontinued.

The hub differs from the 1966 style by having a keyed spline (not visible under the nut), and anchor blocks for the padded cap.

Again a simulated wood Deluxe Steering Wheel option, not a part of the Tilt-Away option, is available. Although similar to the 1966 style, it is not interchangable due to differences at the hub (left).

The standard Fastback 2+2 rear seat is non-folding.

Two seat back latches, one on each side, are used with the folding rear seat. No escutcheon plates (page 115) are provided.

The new Sport Deck Option is an extra cost item, and provides a folding rear seat (previously standard) in the Fastback 2+2.

The Full Width Front Seat, featuring a folding center arm rest, is a continuing option.

The standard adjustable Deep Foam Bucket Seats feature an upholstery pattern which is changed slightly to give more apparent depth to the seat.

The Hardtop rear quarter panels are textured metal in standard trim but padded with Interior Decor Group.

Only in the Convertible are rear seat arm rests and ash trays furnished, but Dealers had similar accessory items available for installation in the Hardtop as early as 1966.

Standard ceiling-mounted Hardtop Courtesy Light is replaced with Overhead Map Light (page 156) in Interior Decor Option.

The luxury dress up Interior Decor Group provides, in addition to the special seat back insert emblem, a chromed trim strip that runs up the sides and over the top of the front seat backs. Along with the seven all-vinyl upholstery choices offered as standard, the Option also offered two additional with "Comfort Weave" patterned seat inserts.

The standard front bucket seats continue to use the 1966 style chromed side trim pieces.

An optional Console, with built-in pockets for the seat belt latches is available, but only with one of the radio options.

The new Select Shift Cruise-O-Matic Drive permits fully automatic or manual shifting through all forward gears. New quadrant sequence is P-R-N-D-2-1.

Console features a built-in ash tray at the rear.

Transmission shift position is displayed on console face.

New for 1967 is the Reversible Key which allows for insertion either way.

Standard transmission shift lever continues with floor-mounted position indicator. Vinyl-covered T-handle is part of Interior Decor Group.

Restyled knobs appear on the instrument panel.

With no suspended air conditioning unit to block it, the optional Console now sweeps nicely upward to blend into the instrument panel.

In addition to this AM radio, other Options include an AM/FM, and an AM/Stereo Tape Player.

Departing from relatively conservative conventional interiors, the new Ford Mustang offered bright, interesting interiors, featuring exciting sports car-like bucket seats and racing type steering wheels.

1964½ Ford Mustang Hardtop

1964½ Mustang Convertible with Mustang accessory wheelcovers

1964½ Hardtop with Ford accessory wire wheelcovers

1965 Mustang Convertible

1965 Mustang Hardtop

1965 Mustang Fastback 2+2

1965 Shelby GT-350

1966 Shelby GT-350

1966 Shelby GT-350H

Shelby GT-350 and
Mustang GT Fastback

1966 Mustang GT Convertible

1966 Mustang GT Hardtop

1966 T-5 Fastback 2+2

1966 Mustang Hardtop

Late in 1965, a new option, the Interior Decor Group, was introduced. Featuring a restyled door panel with integral armrests and special hardware, an embossed seat back panel displayed prancing horses, lending the name "pony interior" to this attractive option.

1966 Mustang GT Fastback 2+2

1967 Mustang Convertible

1967 Mustang Hardtop

1967 Mustang Hardtop

1967 Shelby GT-500 Fastback 2+2

1968 Shelby Cobra 500 KR Convertible

1968 Shelby Cobra GT 500 Fastback 2+2

1968 Mustang 2+2 Fastback

Car has after-market accessory wheels

1968 Mustang GT/CS

1968 Mustang Fastback 2+2 with GT Equipment Group option

1969 Mustang Sports Roof

1970 Mustang Boss 302

1969 Mustang Hardtop with vinyl roof and deluxe wheelcover options

1970 Mustang Grande

1969 Mustang Boss 302

1969 Shelby GT 350 Sports Roof

1971 Mustang Grande

1971 Mustang Boss 351

1972 Mustang Hardtop

1972 Mustang Mach 1

1973 Mustang Convertible

A distinctive molded stitch pattern is featured on the lip of the instrument panel padding.

The Radios are mounted directly into the instrument panel, but without the optional Console (previous page) they appear more obvious.

The optional SelectAire Conditioner is, for the first time, mounted behind the panel and suitable vents provided. The controls for this unit (left) replace the standard heater control panel (far left).

The heater-defroster is standard equipment and an allowance is made if deleted by purchaser.

A new dual hydraulic brake system with separate lines to front and rear brakes is standard. Power Front Disc Brake is a new option.

Although the standard scissors jack is unchanged, its handle is simplified and the rachet (page 113) eliminated.

The standard instrument panel finish is grained. Instruments are black-faced to match. A warning light over the ammeter glows if either half of the new Dual Hydraulic Brake System fails.

Standard speedometer shows maximum 120 mph.

This dual-function instrument matches the speedometer in size.

A brushed-aluminum instrument panel trim is part of the Interior Decor Group option.

The electric clock, optional with standard interior, is a feature of the Interior Decor Group.

Fuel Level (far left) and Temperature gauges are unchanged with selection of optional Tachometer (below)

An optional Trip Odometer (in speedomer) with integral reset button replaces standard unit.

The 0-6000 rpm Tachometer, available option with the V-8 engines, has warning lights built in (at bottom) for oil pressure and charging functions, and replaces the dual-function gauge shown above. An 8000 rpm instrument was also offered.

In this view, the standard 1967 Instrument Panel layout is reminiscent of an over-sized 1966 Rally Pac.

The standard glove compartment is now placed at the lower part of the panel, and above it is a trim plate matching that on the instrument panel.

Just below the new Mustang emblem trim plate can be seen a portion of the new instrument panel padding. This is another part of Ford's "Built In Safety" program in which such padding was added here and at the windshield pillars. The padding was continued into early 1968, and then eliminated.

1967

Available only with one of the four V-8 engines, the GT Equipment Group adds fog lights, F70-14 Wide-Oval Sports type tires, front power disc brakes, and the Special Handling Package which includes stiffer springs, shocks and front stabilizer bar. At the rear, the low-restriction dual-exhaust system terminates (with the two larger engines only) in a pair of dual exhaust tips.

Manual transmission models have GT designation; those with optional Selectshift Cruise-O-Matic are GTA (for Automatic). The GTA designation is used only in 1967.

Fog lamps are added to special grill ornament in GT Equipment Group.

The lamps are same as earlier style, but are set in longer grill bars to match the wider 1967 grill.

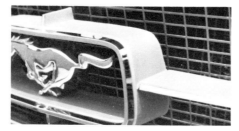

The center portion of the grill emblem is the same on all 1967 models, but the horizontal bars are changed to provide fog lamp support.

1967 fog lamp support bars are longer than earlier styles and extend beyond lamps to fill the wider grill.

1967 Mustang GT Hardtop

All GT (GTA) Mustangs have side stripes in either red, blue, or white. An additional Reflective Group Option adds both reflective stripes and reflective paint on optional Styled Steel Wheels or Deluxe wheel covers if used.

A pair of dual-tipped exhaust pipes exit under a special rear lower valance panel with either of the two larger engines.

Mr. Charlie Jones, Nashville, Georgia

Carroll Shelby Presents The Road Cars...
G.T. 350 and G.T. 500 for 1967

SHELBY G.T.
350 and 500
The Road Cars

1967 Shelby-American GT 500

Introduced on the 1967 models, the distinctive centered fog lights caused cooling problems and later in the model year were spaced at the ends of the grill.

Production of the 1967 Shelby GT 350 and GT 500 commenced in October of 1966 at Los Angeles, but a transfer was made during 1967, and by August all assembly was being done under Ford's supervision in Ironia, Michigan. Early-year advertisement (above) resembles other Shelby-American ads; later, advertising for the cars reflected more polished layouts then current in Ford's other advertisements.

Order your Mustang as hot as you like

...even Shelby hot!

MUSTANG

The earlier GT 350 designation was continued on the vehicle incorporating the 289 cid High Performance engine as modified by Shelby-American, but a new designation, the GT 500 (which supposedly sounded "right" for the car) was used on those incorporating the larger Ford 428 cubic inch 355 horsepower engine.

Mr. Stanley Clapper, Clinton, Wisconsin

SPECIFICATIONS

Both the 1967 Shelby GT 350 and GT 500 are designed and built to provide impeccable handling, performance and braking. They are true GT (gran turismo) cars, capable of transporting four people, or two people and a large quantity of luggage, long distances at high average speeds. Although their engines are Shelby modified for extra high performance, they are completely docile in normal traffic.

ENGINE SPECIFICATIONS: GT 500

Cobra OHV 428 cu. in. 90° V-8; 355 advertised horsepower @ 5400 rpm; 420 lbs./foot of torque @ 3200 rpm; 4.13" x 3.984" bore and stroke; compression ratio 10.50:1; two 4-bbl Holley carburetors (600 cfm flow rate, each); special high-rev hydraulic valve train and camshaft; die cast, polished aluminum "Cobra" rocker arm covers and air cleaner; dual exhaust system.

GT 350

Cobra OHV 289 cu. in. 90° V-8; 306 bhp @ 6000 rpm; 329 lbs./foot of torque @ 4200 rpm; 4.005" x 2.87" bore and stroke; compression ratio 10.50:1; Cobra hi-rise intake manifold with Holley 4-bbl carburetor (715 cfm flow rate); solid valve lifters; die cast, polished aluminum "Cobra" rocker arm covers and air cleaner; dual exhaust system.

GENERAL SPECIFICATIONS: GT 500 AND GT 350

Wheelbase: 108.0"

Tread: Front, 58.0"; Rear, 58.0"

Length: 186.6"

Width: 70.9"

Height: 51.6"

Curb weight: GT 500, 3286 lbs.; GT 350, 2723 lbs.

Distribution, front/rear:

GT 500: 56.4% F, 43.6% R

GT 350: 53.0% F, 47.0% R

Body type: 2-door fastback

Construction: Platform type unitized construction with reinforced floor side members and export front end reinforcement.

Styling: Front, 3.0" extended reinforced fiberglas nose, custom grille with 30% more frontal cooling area. Quad headlights, highbeams inset in grille. Custom fiberglas hood with sculptured airscoop. LeMans locking pins. Sides; functional brake airscoops set in rear quarter sculpturing, LeMans air extractors in rear quarters of roof incorporating advanced safety lights. Rear; sculptured air spoiler across rear deck, full-width taillights. Side striping with model designation above rocker panels.

Suspension: Front; independent, with coil springs and ball joints, Shelby-modified for flatter cornering. .94" diameter front stabilzer bar. Rear; 4-leaf springs with special rebound dampers to control rear spring windup.

Spring rates:

500: 360 lbs./in. front, 135 lbs./in. rear

350: 320 lbs./in. front, 135 lbs./in. rear

Shock absorbers: Tubular, heavy-duty adjustable, factory preset for most driving conditions.

Transmission: Fully synchronized four-speed manual (31 spline for 500, 28 spline for 350) standard.

Ratios: First—2.32:1
Second—1.69:1
Third—1.29:1
Top—1.00:1
Reverse—2.32:1

Heavy-duty Cruise-O-Matic transmission optional. Shift handle lockout prevents skipping or missed shifts when hand-selecting gears.

Ratios: First—2.46:1
Second—1.46:1
Top—1.00:1
Reverse—2.20:1

Final drive: Heavy-duty rear axle with straddle-mounted deep offset drive pinion. Standard ratios:

500—Manual transmission 3.50:1
Automatic transmission 3.25:1

350—Manual transmission 3.89:1
Automatic transmission 3.50:1

Steering: Recirculating ball and nut, linkage-type power assist provides crisp 16-to-1 overall steering ratio*, 37.16 foot turning diameter.

Wheels, tires: Shelby 15" steel wheel with 6.5" rim width. "Speedway 350" low profile 4-ply nylon E70-15 tires designed especially for Shelby GT cars.

Brakes: Front; disc, 11.3", with high speed linings. Rear; 10" x 2.5" cast iron drum, self adjusting. 191.0 sq. in. effective lining area. Independent service brake operating rear drum brakes.

Interior appointments: Deluxe interior with front bucket seats, sculptured folding rear seat*providing carpeted luggage deck. Full instrumentation including 8000 rpm tachometer, 140 mph speedometer, ammeter, oil pressure, water temperature, fuel, Integral roll bar (meets competition requirements). Inertia reel front shoulder harnesses,* seat belts front and rear, padded dashboard, and sun visors.

These specifications were in effect at the time of printing. In the interest of constant product improvement, Shelby American, Inc. reserves the right to add, alter or delete equipment or options, or to change specifications at any time without notice and without incurring obligation. *Optional at extra cost

183

New fiberglass hood features a dual-channel air intake scoop. Lanyard-equipped pin locks are standard.

"Lemans" air extractors, set in the roof quarters, were designed also to hold rear-pointing tail lights, but these were eliminated before production began.

Functional scoops direct cooling air over rear brake assembly. The plastic door edge guard above it is an owner-addition.

The 1967 models have a three inch fiberglass front extension which greatly changes the car's appearance. Center-mounted lights restrict cooling flow through the radiator.

A Shelby GT 500 or GT 350 insignia appears above the appropriate side stripe.

A fiberglass rear deck lid and matching fender end caps greatly change the appearance of the rear, adding to the effect of the wide tail lights.

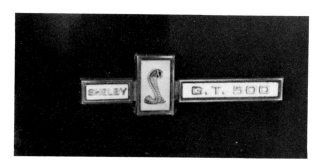

The appropriate Shelby GT 350/500 emblem appears on the rear and also on the instrument panel.

The fiberglass rear deck lid has an interesting built-in air spoiler.

The tail-lights of the GT 350 and GT 500 are derived from the same assemblies that were used on the 1965 Thunderbird.

Large, low-restriction exhaust tips exit under the chrome-trimmed access holes in the lower rear valance panel.

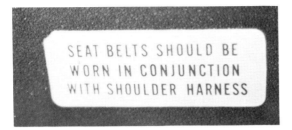

Shoulder harnesses were an option, and when supplied, this label was placed on the sun visor.

Shelby cap appears at the hub of the sports type steering wheel. Horn is blown by depressing center.

A pod containing an Ammeter and an Oil Pressure gauge is furnished since the standard tachometer (below) deleted these instruments originally supplied in the Mustang (page 178).

A 140 mph speedometer, complete with trip odometer, replaces the 120 mph Mustang instruments.

The 8000 rpm tachometer is standard for both vehicles.

A new data plate replaces the style used earlier (page 79).

The roll bar is standard in both models, but the shoulder harness is an option.

The fender cross-brace is eliminated but the cowl-to-shock tower Export brace is retained.

Original GT 500 valve covers have the words "Cobra Le Mans" on single line as seen here; replacement covers (on engine above), still available from Ford, do not.

MUSTANG
1968
...better ideas in action

Having been restyled in 1967, Mustang for 1968 emphasized its new equipment and optional offerings rather than a changed appearance. Among many new items available were an AM/FM Stereo radio, a rear window defogger for the Hardtop and Fastback, re-designed floating-caliper power front disc brakes, and others, but the big news was a brand new engine option for the car. The 302 CID, 4-V carb., 230 horsepower engine was to replace the Challenger Special 289 of former years, and by December of 1967, even the smaller 2-V Challenger 289 was replaced by a 2-V version of the 302. The obsolescent 289 CID engine was then discontinued as a Mustang Option.

Initially the 390 CID Thunderbird Special V-8 engine, rated at 325 HP, and an even larger 427 CID Cobra V-8 with 390 HP were offered, but by the end of December, the larger engine was discontinued entirely and the 390 Option limited to use with the GT Equipment Group.

Mustang Sprint, a specially equipped Hardtop with distinctive trim, was offered as a promotional effort starting late in 1967.

Only Mustang makes it happen!

In the Spring of 1968, Ford revived their humorous 1965 advertising approach with "Sidney Spent Sundays seashelling at the seashore".

1968 MUSTANG SPECIFICATIONS

This catalog will tell you all about three models of the new Mustang. If you're interested in trailering with a new Mustang, your Ford Dealer has another booklet which is yours for the asking. It's called the "1968 Ford Car & Truck Recreation Brochure." Sixteen pages in length, it includes numerous illustrations, facts and suggestions about trailer towing with a '68 car from Ford.

Color and Upholstery Selections: Pick your favorite color from 16 brilliant Super Diamond Lustre Enamel finishes. You have a total of 28 all-vinyl interiors. Your Ford Dealer will be happy to show you his special color and upholstery book. In it are actual paint and upholstery trim samples to let you "try on" various selections with your favorite Mustang model.

Engines (see chart for availability): 200-cu. in. Six—115 hp; 3.68" bore x 3.13" stroke; 8.8 to 1 comp. ratio; 7 main bearings; reg. fuel; single-barrel carb.; auto. choke; self-adj. valves with hydraulic lifters.

289-cu. in. Challenger V-8—195 hp; 4.00" bore x 2.87" stroke; 8.7 to 1 comp. ratio; reg. fuel; 2-barrel carb.; auto. choke; self-adj. valves with hydraulic lifters.

302-cu. in. (five-liter) V-8—230 hp; 4.00" bore x 3.00" stroke; 10.0 to 1 comp. ratio; prem. fuel; 4-barrel carb.; auto. choke; self-adj. valves with hydraulic lifters; dual exhausts.

390-cu. in. Thunderbird Special V-8—325 hp; 4.05" bore x 3.78" stroke; 10.5 to 1 comp. ratio; prem. fuel; 4-barrel carb.; auto. choke; self-adj. valves; oil cap'y, including filter, 5 qt.; dual exhausts.

427-cu. in. Cobra V-8—390 hp; 4.23" bore x 3.78" stroke; 10.9 to 1 comp. ratio; prem. fuel; 4-barrel carb.; auto. choke; self-adjusting valves; oil cap'y, including filter, 5 qt.; dual exhausts. (Available only with GT Group.)

For sedan racing, available late in 1967 on special order only: 302-cu. in. V-8— 345 hp; 4.00" bore x 3.00" stroke; 11.0 to 1 comp. ratio; prem. fuel; special high performance fuel induction system; solid valve lifters; oil cap'y, including filter, 5 qt.; dual exhausts. Available with 4-speed transmission and GT Group only.

Engine Features: 6000-mile (or 6-month) full-flow disposable-type oil filter; replaceable dry element air cleaner; 190° thermostat; 12-volt electrical system with 38-amp. alternator; 42-amp. alternator or High Performance V-8; 54-plate, 45 amp-hr battery; weatherproof ignition; positive-engagement starter; fully aluminized muffler and tailpipe. All engines are electronically mass-balanced for long-lived smoothness.

Transmissions (see chart for availability):

Synchro-Smooth Drive: Synchronized manual shifting in all three forward gears; clash-free downshifting to low while under way. Floor-mounted stick, standard "H" pattern.

4-Speed Manual: Sports-type close-ratio transmission, synchronized in all forward gears; floor-mounted stick.

SelectShift Cruise-O-Matic Drive: Lets you drive fully automatic or shift manually through the gears. Three forward speeds, one reverse. Effective engine braking in low gear (1) for better control on grades and hills. Quadrant sequence (P-R-N-D-2-1).

Rear Axle: Semi-floating hypoid rear axle; straddle-mounted drive pinion (V-8's). Permanently lubricated wheel bearings.

Front Suspension: Angle-Poised Ball-Joint type with coil springs mounted on upper arms. 36,000-mile or (3-year) lube intervals. Strut-stabilized lower arms. Link-type, rubber-bushed ride stabilizer.

Rear Suspension: Longitudinal, 4-leaf springs with rubber-bushed front mounts, compression-type shackles at rear. Asymmetrical, variable-rate design with rear axle located forward of spring centers for anti-squat on takeoff. Diagonally mounted shock absorbers.

Steering: Recirculating ball-type steering gear provides easy handling. Permanently lubricated steering linkage joints. Overall steering ratio 25.4 to 1 (power steering 20.3 to 1). Turning diameter 38 ft.

Brakes: New dual hydraulic brake system with dual master cylinder, separate lines to front and rear brakes. Self-adjusting, self-energizing design. Composite drums grooved for extra cooling: 9" (Six), 10" (V-8's). Total lining areas: 131 sq. in. (Six), 154 sq. in. (V-8's).

Tires: Tubeless, blackwall with Tyrex rayon cord, 4-ply rating. Safety rim wheels. Tire size—6.95 x 14.

Dimensions & Capacities: Length 183.6"; width 70.9"; height: hardtop 51.6", fastback 51.6", convertible 51.4"; wheelbase 108"; treads 58.5"; trunk luggage volume (cu. ft.): hardtop 9.3, convertible 6.8 (top down), fastback 5.6 (18.5 with optional rear seat folded down); fuel 17 gal.

Approximate Weights: Mustang Hardtop, 2797 lb. (Six), 2985 lb. (V-8); Mustang Fastback 2+2, 2824 lb. (Six), 3012 lb. (V-8); Mustang Convertible, 2924 lb. (Six), 3112 lb. (V-8).

12 MUSTANG POWER TEAMS

ENGINES	TRANSMISSIONS		
	3-Speed Manual Trans.	SelectShift Cruise-O-Matic Drive	4-Speed Manual Trans.
200-cu. in. Six	Std.	Opt.	N.A.
289-cu. in. Challenger V-8	Std.	Opt.	Opt.
302-cu. in. Challenger Special V-8	Std.	Opt.	Opt.
302-cu. in. High Performance V-8*	N.A.	N.A.	Opt.
390-cu. in. Thunderbird Special V-8	N.A.	Opt.	Opt.
427-cu. in. Cobra V-8	N.A.	Opt.	N.A.

*Available on special order only.

1968 Mustang Fastback 2+2

Many owners "customized" their cars with readily available accessories. This car has Keystone wheels, one of those contempory after-market accessories.

Mrs. Marylou Curtis, Oceanside, California

The grill emblem is simplified and an inner trim strip added to emphasize lines of the grill opening.

The Mustang "corral" is reduced in thickness and now is barely more than a ring around the running horse.

Single headlamps are used; original equipment has FOMOCO insignia.

Bright metal grill opening and hood lip trim is continued.

Initially standard equipment, the front and rear bumper guards shortly became optional equipment when they were joined with the wheelhousing lip moldings as a new Option.

Initially standard, the louvered hood became an Option early in the model year and a plain hood (below) was furnished as standard equipment.

The familiar F-O-R-D at the hood lip (page 149) is deleted starting in 1968.

The optional louvered hood has built-in turn signal indicators (page 149).

Dual windshield wipers and washers are continuing standard equipment for 1968.

Side marker lights in front (and reflectors in the rear) are now standard equipment and provide a quick identification reference.

The new "yield-away" inside rear view mirror is suspended directly from the windshield and the former bracket omitted.

1967 view shown for comparison.

The engine choice (other than the SIX) is again made a part of the side emblem.

Although there is little visible difference, the 1968 windshield glass does not interchange with any other due to minor differences in configuration.

A script style lettering is used for the first time, replacing the former block letters (page 150).

The rocker panel molding is standard equipment on the Fastback and the Convertible.

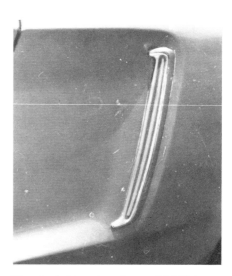

The dual side trim pieces of 1967 (page 150) are replaced with a simplified trim.

The standard rear window of the Hardtop is plain; that on the Fastback tinted, and the Convertible has a two-pane folding glass rear window as standard equipment.

The two groups of three individual tail lights are continued unchanged from 1967.

The Bright Deck Lid and Quarter Panel Extension Moldings are standard equipment on all 1968 models.

Rear side marker reflectors are new standard equipment in 1968 (left). Those on the GT Models (and the GT 350 and GT 500) have chromed frames (above).

Resembling the previous style (page 154), standard inside door panel has a new horizontal rib pattern and a wider sweep to its bright metal trim strip.

Newly restyled window riser crank is used on both standard and luxury interiors.

The optional door panel has molded-in arm rest, door pull strap, and courtesy lights set behind a decorative grill.

Positive door lock buttons are continued; inside door handles cannot override a depressed button.

Separate arm rests with integral door pulls are used on the standard door panel.

New for 1968 is the folding inside door handle which is used on all models.

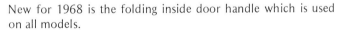

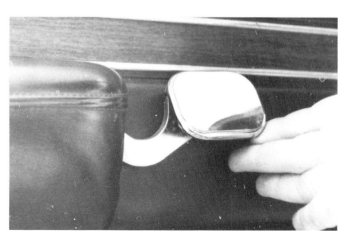

Silent-Flo Ventilation is continued in the Fastback 2+2 as standard equipment.

Two latches are furnished with the optional folding rear seat. Escutcheon plate resembles the 1965/66 style (page 58) but has a wider skirt.

The fixed rear seat of the Fastback is standard. The Option this year is called (correctly) a "Folding Rear Seat", not a misleading "Sport Deck" as it was in 1967.

A new feature for 1968 is the locking seat back. This lever releases the latch.

Pleats on the 1968 seats run lengthwise; those on the 1967 seats run crosswise (page 156).

Again a bench front seat is offered, the upholstery having correct 1968 pattern.

1968

One of the new standard 1968 "Lifeguard Design Features" is a new energy absorbing steering column (above), and new two-spoke steering wheel. The Mustang emblem appears at the hub (upper left).

As part of the Interior Decor Group, a wood-grained trim is used on the instrument panel, and extends onto the heater/defroster control panel (below). Standard finish is shown at left.

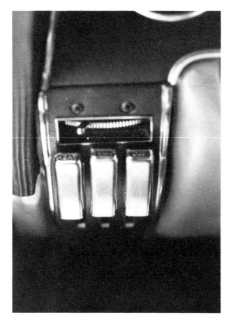

Optional SelectAire Conditioner is installed with this Control Panel replacing standard Heater/Defroster controls (right).

A running change in 1968 saw the replacement of the earlier-style radio antenna (left) with this rectangular unit.

This is the last year for this transmission shift indicator. A new style will appear in the 1969 model.

Optional SelectShift Cruise-O-Matic allows automatic shifting or manual shifting through the gears without a clutch pedal.

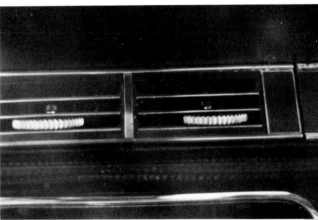

Until December the 1968 models continued to receive the instrument panel and windshield pillar padding used in 1967; after that these items were discontinued (right).

In addition to this optional AM radio, there were also optional AM/FM Stereo (for the first time) and Stereo-Sonic Tape System with AM radios. The latter two were installed with in-door speakers.

Optional SelectAire Conditioner installation adds outlets at center and ends of instrument panel.

Standard five dial instrument panel is finished in black.

The Interior Decor Group Option adds wood-grained trim on panel. New for 1968 is the arrow-shaped wiper control cutout replacing the 1967 rectangle (page 178).

An optional sweep second hand electric clock is also included in the Interior Decor Group Option. When installed, it replaces the blanking instrument (below center).

An Oil Pressure gauge replaces the Gasoline Gauge that was used here on the 1967 model (page 178).

High Beam Indicator for 1968 is a lighted pony.

Location of the Temperature Gauge is unchanged.

The standard 120 MPH speedometer is red-lined at 70 MPH, and a matching instrument has dual Fuel and Alternator gauges. The earlier 1967 instrument (page 178) had dual *Oil Pressure* and Alternator units.

An optional 140 MPH speedometer with trip odometer and integral reset knob is offered, as well as an 8000 RPM Tachometer.

An enterprising Detroit manufacturer offered a Mustang rear deck lid conversion kit at only $169.95 which provided added seating for two more passengers and a "continental"-styled deck-mounted spare wheel. A similar accessory had been offered over ten years earlier by a California accessories manufacturer as the "Birdnest" for the two-passenger Thunderbirds, but the popularity of both appears to have reached similarly low levels.

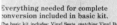

A new tapered style GT stripe appears in 1968, but the old rocker-panel style was also used if requested.

The GT Equipment Group option included fog lamps, a dual exhaust system with special "quad" outlets, the unique GT stripe (either style, see above), the heavy-duty suspension including stiffer springs and shocks and heavier front stabilizer bar, wide-oval tires with special GT styled steel wheels, and the GT flip-open gas cap, but power front disc brakes were a separate added option (required with the larger engines).

1968 MUSTANG GT FASTBACK 2+2

A GT nameplate is affixed to the front fender skirts.

The customary GT fog lamps are not provided with horizontal support bars as previously (page 180).

Mr. Patrick Girault, Oceanside, California

The 1968 foglamps resemble the earlier ones, but they differ in that they are designed to be suspended from above their center line rather than supported from beneath it as with the earlier horizontal fog lamp bars. Thus, they would be "upside down" if used in the 1965-67 installations. Although the bulb can be rotated to appear correctly, an indexing hole which should be at the bottom can be detected at the top.

The newly restyled GT tapered body side stripe emphasizes the lines of the Fastback 2+2.

The familiar data plate still appears on the left front door in its accustomed position, but beginning in 1968, the Vehicle Identification Number was also placed on the instrument panel. At this time it was located on the *right* side not the left as it was later.

The special tapered GT stripe is used along with the standard side trim.

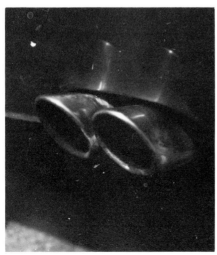

A GT flip-open, fast action gas cap (page 303) is furnished with the GT Equipment Group as is a special low-restriction dual exhaust system terminated in chromed dual "quad" exhaust tips.

1968 Mustang GT/CS

Not infrequently a regional Dealer's Group will promote a "limited edition" of the product as a special event. One such was the 1968 promotion of the Mustang GT/CS by the Southern California Ford Dealers.

The "California Special" was a standard 1968 Mustang Hardtop specially outfitted with several dress-up trim items. Among these were a blackout grill, rectangular fog lights, the functional louvered hood, special striping effects, side air scoops, wide tail lights, rear deck lid with built-in spoiler, and a pop-open gas cap.

The GT/CS promotion was limited to under 5000 units. Among its most distinctive features may well have been its name since other than trim items, the car had no special handling or engine modifications.

1968 GT/CS

Non-functioning decorative side air scoops resemble those on the Shelby cars.

Mr. Glen Erickson, Oceanside, California

The 1968 Optional hood is standard on the GT/CS, and includes the built-in turn signals.

Rectangular fog lights replace the standard trim on the blacked-out grill of the GT/CS.

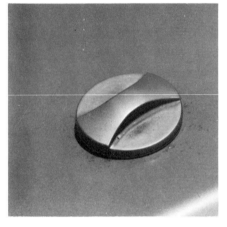

Turnscrew hood locks are a standard dress-up feature added on the GT/CS.

The conventional Mustang script trim on the sides is standard.

These Lucas fog lamps are a part of the dress-up equipment installed on the Mustang GT/CS.

The special side trim stripe, side scoops and rocker panel molding are all standard equipment on this model.

The appearance at the rear is greatly changed by the added spoiler and tail lights as well as by the special paint stripes emphasizing the emphasizing paint stripes.

The basic California Special Mustang GT/CS proved to be an excellent and well-received promotion. Most were sold heavily equipped with added Options such as one of the V-8 engines, SelectAire Conditioning, full wheelcovers or Styled Steel Wheels, Interior Decor Group, Cruise-O-Matic transmission, etc.

All things considered, they were basically attractive, and when equipped with some of the many available Options, they became especially interesting variants.

The special rear deck lid with its built-in spoiler is provided with appropriately shaped fender end-caps for fully coordinated effect. Script nameplates are placed on the rear fenders above the standard side markers.

The script Mustang nameplate is repeated on the rear deck lid.

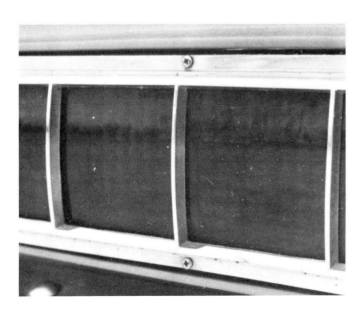

The wide rear tail lights are identical with those used on the 1965 Thunderbird. However, in this application, the sequential signal concept is not used.

1968 SHELBY GT 350/500

Only Mustang and Carroll Shelby could make this happen!

This being a Mustang based Shelby GT convertible with 428 cubic inch power, it has to be the mother of all rag tops! The others are pale children by comparison. Just try and get things like a built-in roll bar on any of the meeker cars and you'll see what we mean.

The reason old Doctor Shelby elected to build his reputation even higher on Mustang is that he knows Mustang is a driver's car. One that goes, stops, and steers. It's the original "designed to be designed by you" car . . . only Mustang has so many performance options. Engines from a base 289 cube V-8 all the way up to that velvet brute . . . the 390. Suspension options run all the way from a main-street ride to something that's able to cope with the banking at Daytona. Tires run the gamut from plain old whitewalls to wide-oval radials. Transmissions? Pick from a 3-speed manual, 4-speed, or 3-cog automatic. This last has a hold feature that lets you hang on to a gear . . . upshift . . . downshift or play it smoothly shiftless. Mustang puts a stop to all this jazz with newly engineered optional front wheel disc brakes.

To start designing your own Mustang see your Ford Dealer now. He'll turn you loose on a Mustang . . . turning yourself on after that shouldn't be hard.

The one car that can't be mistaken for any other.

FORD . . . has a better idea.

For the first (and only) time, the Cobra name was actually applied to the Mustang-based Shelbys, and for 1968 they became the Shelby Cobra GT 350 (with standard 302 CID engine or with an optional supercharger) and the Shelby Cobra GT 500 (with standard Cobra 428 cid engine; optional 400 horsepower Cobra 427 cid engine). Then, later in the year, after the 427 engine had been discontinued as a Mustang option, the 500KR, promoted as the "King of the Road" appeared featuring the Cobra Jet 428 with a larger carburetor and revised distributor curve. Both the GT 500KR and the GT 350 were available either as a Fastback, or for the first time, in a Convertible model.

1968 Shelby Cobra 500KR Convertible

Mr. Michael Pores, LaJolla, Californi

1968 Shelby Cobra GT 500 Fastback

Mr. Larry Evenson, Pleasant Hill, California

All 1968 Shelby Cobras had as standard equipment, the Mustang Interior Decor Group Option with its deluxe interior trim and walnut-grained appliques on doors and instrument panel.

ENGINE SPECIFICATIONS: GT 500
Standard: All new Cobra OHV 428 cu. in. V-8; 360 horsepower @ 5400 rpm; 420 lbs./foot of torque @ 3200 rpm; 4.13" x 3.984" bore and stroke; compression ratio 10.5:1; hydraulic valve lifters. Cobra high velocity high volume intake manifold with advanced design, 4 bbl Holley carburetor with 600 CFM (flow rate) primaries, 715 CFM secondaries. High capacity fuel pump.

Optional*: All new Cobra hydraulic OHV 427 cu. in. V-8; 400 horsepower @ 5600 rpm; 460 lbs./foot of torque @ 3200 rpm; 4.235" x 3.788" bore and stroke; compression ratio 11.6:1; hydraulic valve lifters, advanced design cathedral float 4 bbl Holley carburetor. High capacity fuel pump.**

GT 350
Standard: All new OHV 302 cu. in. V-8; 250 horsepower @ 4800 rpm; 310 lbs./foot of torque @ 2800 rpm; 4.0" x 3.0" bore and stroke; compression ratio 10.5:1; hydraulic valve lifters. Cobra high volume high velocity intake manifold with 4 bbl carburetor with 600 CFM flow rate.
Optional*: Cobra centrifugal supercharger, 335 horsepower @ 5200 rpm; 325 lbs./foot cf torque @ 3200 rpm.†
NOTE: All Cobra GT engines include high velocity high flow intake manifolds, die-cast aluminum rocker covers, low restriction oval design diecast aluminum air cleaner, chromed filler caps, high capacity fuel pumps.

GENERAL SPECIFICATIONS:
Body types: 2-door fastback and convertible. Full unitized construction.

Wheelbase: 108.0"
Tread: Front, 58.1"; Rear, 58.1"
Length: 186.81"
Width: 70.9"
Height: Fastback, 51.8"

††**Curb weight:** 350 (302 engine, autom. transm.); fastback 3146 lbs.
500 (428 engine, autom. transm.); fastback, 3445 lbs.

††**Weight distribution:** 350: 53% F,
(Fastback) 47% R.
500: 56.4% F, 43.6% R.
††Estimated design weights

Suspension
Front: Independent with coil springs and ball joints. Spring rates; 320 lbs./in. (350), 360 lbs./in. (500). Front stabilizer bar, .94" diameter. Extra capacity telescopic double acting tubular adjustable shock absorbers.
Rear: 4-leaf semi-elliptic springs with extra capacity telescopic double acting tubular adjustable shock absorbers and custom windup dampers. Rate: 135 lbs./in. (350 and 500).

Steering: Recirculating ball and nut with hydraulic power assist. Steering ratio 16:1; 37.16' turning circle.

Brakes: Front, floating caliper power assisted ventilated 11.3" discs with high performance pads; rear drums 10" x 1.75" size with high performance linings. Dual master cylinder with low pressure warning light. Effective lining area: 180.0 sq. in.

Wheels: 15" safety type steel wheel, 6" rim width with diecast cover standard.

Tires: 15" Goodyear Speedway 350 E70 true 4 ply, nylon, wide path tires are designed for this car, 130 mph test standard.

Transmission: Fully synchronized four-speed manual standard.
Ratios: First—2.32:1
Second - 1.69:1
Third—1.29:1
Top—1.00:1
Reverse—2.32:1
Heavy-duty, close-coupled, automatic transmission optional. Shift handle detent minimizes skipping or missed shifts when hand-selecting gears.
Ratios: First—2.46:1
Second—1.46:1
Top—1.00:1
Reverse—2.20:1

Final drive: Heavy-duty rear axle with straddle-mounted large diameter ring gear and deep offset drive pinion. Standard ratios:
500—Manual transmission 3.50:1
Automatic transmission 3.50:1
350—Manual transmission 3.89:1
Automatic transmission 3.50:1

Safety Features: Padded instrument panel, sun visors, steering wheel center, sun visors. Impact-absorbing collapsible steering column. Seat back retaining latches, padded front seat backs, safety door and regulator handles. Seat belts front and rear. Advanced design front seat shoulder harnesses with improved inertia reels (dual style in fastback, diagonal style in convertible). Padded high-strength steel 1½"

diameter integral overhead safety bar. Sequential turn signals, front safety marker lights, rear quarter marker reflectors.
Styling, Appointments
Exterior: Precision moulded custom fiberglass hood and front assembly incorporates dual air intake scoops, functional louvered extractors. Custom self retained push-and-turn hood locks with additional retaining cables. Rectangular fog lights mounted in grille opening. Rolled section lightweight moldings on grille and wheel openings. Le Mans type air extractors on rear quarters of roof (fastback only). Brake air scoops set in lower rear quarters. Precision moulded custom fiberglass trunk deck lid with integral air spoiler. GT stripe on lower rocker panels.
Interior: Deluxe all-vinyl interior with bucket seats, full loop pile carpeting, matching custom styled console with padded armrest glove box with rear ash tray and courtesy light, walnut-grained appliques on instrument panel and door panels. Full instrumentation; 8000 rpm tachometer, 140 mph speedometer, oil pressure, ammeter, water temperature, fuel gauge, electric clock (supercharger pressure and fuel pressure if supercharged). Folding rear seat* with retractable safety luggage retaining bar (fastback only), tie-down loops on safety bar (convertible only).
These specifications were in effect at the time of printing. In the interest of constant product improvement, Shelby Automotive, Inc. reserves the right to add, alter or delete equipment or options, or to change specifications at any time without notice and without incurring obligation.

*Extra-cost option
**Not available with manual transmission
†Not available with air conditioning

211

1968 SHELBY GT 350/500

New moulded fiberglass hood has dual air intake scoops in front and functional extractor louvers at the rear.

Rectangular fog lamps differ from GT/CS as does the expanded-metal grill

Hood latches are turn-screw type as used on the GT/CS (page 208).

The data plate reads "Shelby Automotive, Inc.", rather than "Shelby American, Inc." as it did on the 1967 model (page 187).

Both the GT 350 and the GT 500 had, in addition to appropriate side striping, a Cobra emblem on the fender skirts just above the stripe.

The front end of the GT 350/500 is extended with special fiberglass assemblies. A unique expanded metal curved grill protects the radiator, and chromed headlight bezels dress up the light.

The Integral Overhead Safety Bar (roll bar) is standard in both models, but more obvious in the Convertible (below).

Used on the Fastback only, these air extractors employ a venturi principle to pull air from the interior.

Side scoops are functional rear brake cooling air intakes.

1968 SHELBY GT 350/500

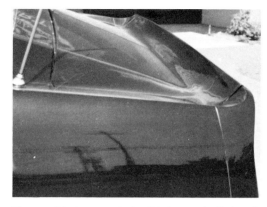

The molded rear deck lid has a built-in air spoiler. Antenna is rear mounted to avoid radio interference due to non-shielding fiberglass hood.

A rectangular chromed reflector frame is used, differing somewhat from the GT item (page 195).

The tail light assembly is identical to that on the 1965 Thunderbird, including its sequential signalling circuit.

S-H-E-L-B-Y appears on the deck lid, and a pop-open gas cap is provided. This is the GT 500 lid; see page 303 for GT 500KR.

All models have low restriction dual exhaust systems, but additional dual "quad" type tips are used on the GT KR's Cobra Jet 428.

The padded arm rest console is standard equipment and contains a built-in glove box, rear ash tray, and courtesy light. An embossed Cobra insignia is featured on its padded surface (below).

A special Shelby Cobra insignia is placed at the hub of the standard two-spoke steering wheel.

The Shelby Cobra data plate resembles standard Ford, but has added "Special Performance Vehicle" designation.

GT 500 door sill plate

GT 500KR door sill plate

A 140 MPH speedometer with integral odometer and reset is standard.

Matching 8000 RPM tachometer replaces standard dual-function instrument (page 201).

A Gasoline gauge replaces standard Oil Pressure unit.

Appropriate insignia (including GT 350) is placed on the standard walnut-grained instrument panel.

Instruments are standard, but the insignia is owner-added.

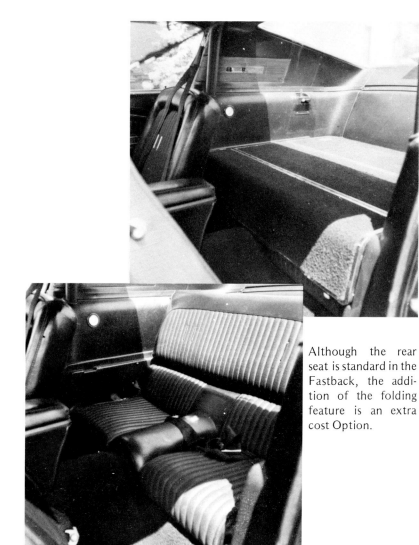

Shoulder harness is standard for both body styles, but the dual strap was used only in the Fastback; Convertible had single diagonal strap.

Although the rear seat is standard in the Fastback, the addition of the folding feature is an extra cost Option.

The standard integral safety bar is a padded 1½" steel tube. Used in both the Fastback and the Convertible, it is formed to allow adequate access to the rear seats.

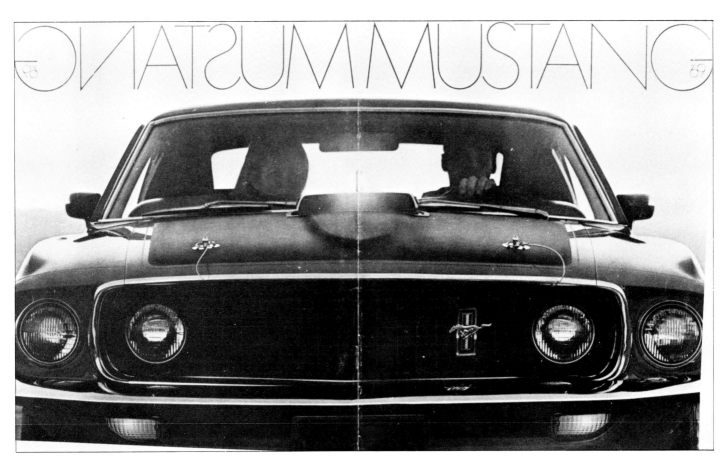

Specifications

1969 brought the first substantial redesign of the Mustang, and with it, some new terminology. Longer by almost four inches, the car, at 187.4" overall, received styling changes that further emphasized its "bigger" look.

The Fastback 2+2 name was gone now, replaced by a new name, the SportsRoof, a new body style complete with rear deck spoiler, vent-less side windows, a new grill, and the quad headlights typical of the 1969 model year.

A variant of the new SportsRoof, the Mach 1, brought special trim and styling as well as GT-type equipment to the body style and was considered to be a separate model. A dressed up Hardtop version having special upholstery and interior trim, was designated the Grande, and as previously, a Convertible was also available.

Color and Upholstery: 16 brilliant Super Diamond Lustre Enamel exterior finishes, and 5 standard vinyl interior trims, 6 optional vinyl trims, 4 cloth and vinyl trims in Grandé, and 3 knitted vinyl trims in Mach I. Ask your Ford Dealer to show you his color and upholstery book and choose your favorite color combinations.

Engines:
200-cu. in. Six—115 hp; 3.68" bore x 3.13" stroke; 8.8 to 1 comp. ratio; 7 main bearings; reg. fuel; single-barrel carb.

250-cu. in. 4.1 Litre Six—155 hp; 3.68" bore x 3.91" stroke; 9.0 to 1 comp. ratio; 7 main bearings; reg. fuel; single-barrel carb.

302-cu. in. V-8—220 hp; 4.00" bore x 3.00" stroke; 9.5 to 1 comp. ratio; reg. fuel; 2-barrel carb.

351-cu. in. V-8—250 hp; 4.00" bore x 3.50" stroke; 9.5 to 1 comp. ratio; reg. fuel; 2-barrel carb.

351-cu. in. V-8—290 hp; 4.00" bore x 3.50" stroke; 10.7 to 1 comp. ratio; prem. fuel; 4-barrel carb.

390-cu. in. V-8—320 hp; 4.05" bore x 3.78" stroke; 10.5 to 1 comp. ratio; prem. fuel; 4-barrel carb.

428-cu. in. V-8—335 hp; 4.13" bore x 3.98" stroke; 10.6 to 1 comp. ratio; prem. fuel; 4-barrel carb.

428-cu. in. Cobra Jet Ram-Air V-8—335 hp; 4.13" bore x 3.98" stroke; 10.6 to 1 comp. ratio; prem. fuel; 4-barrel carb.

Engine Features: 6000-mile (or 6-month) maintenance schedule with full-flow disposable-type oil filter; dry element air cleaner; auto. choke; self-adjusting valves with hydraulic lifters; 12-volt electrical system; 42-amp. alternator; 45 amp-hr battery with 200 through 390 CID engines; 55-amp. alternator and 80 amp-hr battery with 428's.

Transmissions:
3-Speed Manual: Fully synchronized 3-speed manual transmission.

4-Speed Manual: Sports-type close- or wide-ratio fully synchronized transmission with short throw.

SelectShift Cruise-O-Matic Drive: 3-speed fully automatic transmission which may be used manually to maintain first or second gear for engine braking or for better control on hills, or when hauling a trailer.

Mustang Power Teams

Engines	Transmissions			
	3-Speed Manual	Select-Shift	4-Speed Manual Wide-Ratio	4-Speed Manual Close-Ratio
200-cu. in. Six	Std.	Opt.	N.A.	N.A.
250-cu. in. Six	Std.	Opt.	N.A.	N.A.
302-cu. in. V-8	Std.	Opt.	Opt.	N.A.
351-cu. in. V-8 (2 bbl.)	Std.	Opt.	Opt.	Opt.
351-cu. in. V-8 (4 bbl.)	Std.	Opt.	Opt.	Opt.
390-cu. in. V-8	N.A.	Opt.	Opt.	Opt.
428-cu. in. V-8	N.A.	Opt.	N.A.	Opt.
428-cu. in. Ram-Air V-8	N.A.	Opt.	N.A.	Opt.

Rear Axle: Semi-floating hypoid type; permanently lubricated rear wheel bearings.

Front Suspension: Angle-Poised Ball-Joint type with coil springs; strut-stabilized lower arms; link-type stabilizer.

Rear Suspension: Asymmetrical variable-rate design longitudinal 4-leaf springs. Diagonally mounted shocks.

Steering: Recirculating ball-type, permanently lubricated. 25.3 to 1 overall ratio (20.3 to 1 power). Turning diameter 37.6'.

Brakes: Dual hydraulic system with dual master cylinder. Self-adjusting, self-energizing design. Lining areas: 131 sq. in. (200 Six): 154.7 sq. in. (250 Six, 302 V-8); 174.2 sq. in. (351, 390 & 428's).

Tires: Base tire size, C78-14, on models with 200-, 250-, and 302-cu.-in. engines. E70-14 wide-oval white sidewalls on Mach I base model. Other tires include: E78-14, F70-14 wide-oval belted white sidewalls, and F70-14 wide-oval belted blackwalls with raised white brand lettering. Tire sizes depend in part on engine choice and other equipment.

Dimensions and Capacities: Length 187.4"; width 71.3"; height 51.3"; wheelbase 108"; treads 58.5"; trunk 9.8 cu.ft. (Hardtop), 5.3 cu. ft. (SportsRoof), 8 cu. ft. (Convertible); fuel 20 gal.

Approximate Weights: (Six) Hardtop 2832 lb., SportsRoof 2856 lb., Convertible 2942 lb.

STANDARD FORD MOTOR COMPANY LIFEGUARD DESIGN SAFETY FEATURES

Every 1969 Mustang includes: Dual Hydraulic Brake System with warning light □ Glare reduced instrument panel padding, windshield wiper arms, steering wheel hub, horn ring, rearview mirror/mirror mounting and windshield pillars □ Energy-absorbing steering column and steering wheel □ Energy-absorbing armrests and safety-designed door handles □ Front and rear lap belts with front outboard retractors □ Turn indicators with lane-changing signal feature □ Inside day/night, yield away rearview mirror □ Energy-absorbing instrument panel with padding □ Padded sun visors □ Two speed or variable speed windshield wipers □ Wind-shield washers □ Double-thick laminate safety glass windshield □ Double-yoke safety door latches and safety hinges □ 4-way emergency flasher □ Back-up lights □ Side marker lights or reflectors □ Energy-absorbing front seat back tops with padding □ Self-locking folding front seat backs □ Shoulder belts for outboard front seat passengers (except convertibles) □ Safety-designed coat hooks □ Safety-designed window regulator knobs □ Safety-designed radio control knobs and push buttons □ Outside rearview mirror, driver's side □ Safety rim wheels and load-rated tires □ Corrosion-resistant brake lines □ Uniform transmission shift quadrant □ Safety design front end structure.

Note: Your new 1969 Mustang comes equipped with factory engineered and approved parts such as the dependable Autolite Sta-Ful battery, Autolite Power-Tip spark plugs, Autolite shock absorbers, and an Autolite 6000-mile oil filter. For continued top performance, be sure to specify genuine Autolite parts whenever replacement is necessary.

While the information shown herein was correct when approved for printing, Ford Division reserves the right to discontinue, or change at any time, specifications or designs without incurring any obligations. Some features shown or described are optional at extra cost.

The 1969 351 CID V-8 engine was offered with 2-V carburetor at 250 horsepower, or with 4-V and higher compression ratio at 290 HP.

The 428 CID engine was developed in 1966 to replace the earlier 390 in the bigger Fords and Thunderbirds. Quiet, and lightweight for its displacement, Ford's performance engineers interchanged some parts from the 427, added some new parts, and came up with the 428 Cobra Jet engine featuring an improved nodular cast-iron block and crankshaft, aluminum pistons and forged steel piston rods. A "Super Cobra Jet" 428 engine with a slightly different lower end selection comes with a standard external oil cooler in front of the radiator, and is supplied with the higher-ratio rear axles.

1969 Mustang Mach I with 428 CID 4V Cobra Jet Ram-Air V-8

Ford's Exclusive Shaker scoop actually protrudes through the hood — rams air directly into the carburetor under full throttle.

Mustang Mach I—Holder of 295 land speed records.

This is the one that Mickey Thompson started with. From its wide-tread, belted radials to its wind tunnel designed SportsRoof, the word is go. There's just one body — the same wind-splitting sheetmetal as the specially modified Mach I that screamed around Bonneville, clocking over 155, hour after hour, to break some 295 USAC speed and endurance records. Underneath that sleek, new shape is more Mustang than ever before. Standard are a new lightweight, free-breathing 2V 351 CID V-8, rated at 250 hp; competition handling suspension, hood scoop, exposed lock pins and matte black hood, chrome styled steel wheels, and white sidewall belted tires. In the high back, bucket seat you sit behind a three-spoke sports steering wheel with integral horn rim switch, and look in dual, color-keyed racing mirrors. Check the complete instrument cluster mounted in the simulated teakwood-grained panel. Shift the fully synchronized manual transmission from the center console. Then and only then, you'll begin to realize what kind of great machine you got for $3122. 1969 Mustang Mach I with 428 CID 4V Cobra Jet Ram-Air V-6, F70 x 14 wide-oval belted tires and 4-speed manual transmission, tach and trip odometer (as illustrated)—$3746.43.*

Mustang GT—Stack extra performance on the Mustang you fancy.

Mustang's all-new GT's come in three sporty shapes—hardtop, convertible and SportsRoof. And all of them have a big slice of the all-out performance that has made our specially prepared Mustangs the big Trans Am gun over many a rough road course. The GT Equipment Group includes styled steel wheels, wide-tread belted white sidewall tires, hood scoop and locking pins, special handling package, racing stripes, and more. Performance comes on strong with the new, lightweight 351 CID 2V 250-hp V-8. And price comes on cool at only $2928.05 Hardtop or SportsRoof GT. (Convertible GT—$214 additional.)*

1969 Mustang GT Hardtop

Mach I Specifications—Standard engine: 351 CID 2V V-8. Bore and stroke, 4.00 x 3.50 in. 9.5:1 compression, regular fuel. 250 hp at 4600 rpm. Torque 355 lbs-ft at 2600 rpm. Optional engines: 351 CID 4V V-8, compression 10.7:1, premium fuel. 290 hp at 4800 rpm. Torque 385 lb. at 3200 rpm. 390 CID 4V V-8 (see page P6). 428 CID 4V V-8 (see page P2). All 4V engines have dual exhausts. Transmissions: Std. 3-speed fully synchronized floor shift, ratios 2.42:1, 1.61:1, 1.00:1. Optional 4-speed floor shift, ratios 2.78:1, 1.93:1, 1.36:1, 1.00:1. Select-shift ratios 2.46:1, 1.46:1, 1.00:1. Brakes: 10.0 in. drums, lining area 173.3 sq. in. Wheelbase: 108.0". Overall length 187.4". Weight 3244 lb. Wheels: Styled steel, 14 x 6 with wide-oval belted sidewall tires. Optional FR70 radial ply. Suspension: GT handling with 351 & 390 CID V-8's, competition HD with 428 CID V-8. Mustang GT Specifications—Standard engine: 351 2V V-8 (see Mach I specifications). Optional engines: 351 4V V-8, 290 hp, 390 CID 4V V-8, 320 hp (see page P2), 428 CID 4V V-8, 335 hp with through-the-hood functional air scoop (see page P2). All 4V engines have dual exhausts. Transmissions: Standard 3-speed fully synchronized floor shift. Ratios 2.42:1, 1.61:1,

1.00:1. Optional 4-speed floor shift, ratios 2.78:1, 1.93:1, 1.36:1, 1.00:1. Select-shift, ratio 2.46:1, 1.46:1, 1.00:1. Brakes: 10.0 in. drums, lining area 173.3 sq. in. Wheelbase: 108.0". Overall length 187.4". Weights: Hardtop—3210 lb. SportsRoof—3244 lb. Convertible—3330 lb. Wheels: Styled steel, 14 x 6 with wide-tread belted tires. Optional FR70 radial ply. Suspension: GT handling with 351 & 390 CID V-8's, competition HD with 428 CID V-8. Mach I and Mustang GT Options: Extra charge over 351 CID V-8: 351 CID 4V V-8 (290 hp)—$25.91, 390 CID 4V V-8 (320 hp)—$99.74, 428 CID 4V V-8 (335 hp)—$224.12 (390 and 428 CID require Cruise-O-Matic or 4-speed manual transmission at extra cost). 428 CID 4V Cobra Jet Ram-Air V-8 (335 hp)—$357.46 (requires Cruise-O-Matic or, close ratio 4-speed manual transmission and, F70x14 wide-oval belted tires at extra cost). Select-Shift Cruise-O-Matic — 351 2V or 4V V-8—$200.85 • 390 4V, 428 4V or 428 CID 4V Cobra Jet V-8—$222.06 • Four-Speed Manual—351 2V or 4V V-8—$204.64—390, 428 and 428 CID Cobra Jet V-8's (includes tach & trip odometer)—$253.92 • Power Steering—$94.95 • Traction-Lok Differential—$63.51 • Power Front Disc Brakes—$64.77 • F70x14 Wide-Oval Belted Black Sidewall Tires with raised white letters—$27.27.*

1969

1969 Mustang Hardtop   *Beach City Motor Company, Oceanside, California*

1969 Mustang SportsRoof

Mr. Donald Penning, Oceanside, California

Smooth, longer, standard hood has built-in windsplit and extends further forward requiring a new latching mechanism (below). See pages 231 and 234 for alternate hood options.

1969 brought a dual quad headlight system in which four sealed beams are used. The inner lights, set in the grill, have effective over-hanging shrouds.

A chromed bezel replaces the painted item used in 1968 (page 192).

New built-in parking lights replace earlier round style.

This Mustang emblem is used on the 1969 grill.

Front side marker lights are continued, but have new shape (page 193).

New windshield is wider and has greater slope providing improved visibility.

The rocker panel is part of an Exterior Decor Group Option which also includes full wheel covers, wheel opening lip moldings and rear deck moldings on the Convertible and Hardtops.

The Mustang script again appears on the front fenders.

Beginning with the 1969 model, the familiar vent panes are omitted from the side windows.

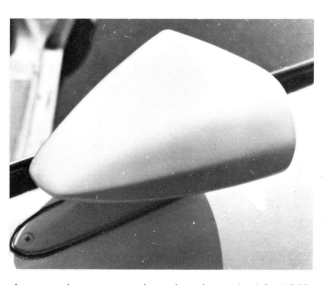

A new racing type rear view mirror is standard for 1969.

1969

A little-known 1969 version, the Mustang 'E' was a variant of the standard SportsRoof claimed to provide greater fuel economy. It was available only with the SIX, a lower rear axle ratio, larger torque converter and an automatic transmission. Air conditioning was not available, but in other respects the "E" was identical to the standard SportsRoof except that a "Mustang E" insignia replaced this standard trim on the quarter panel.

The rear window of the new SportsRoof model is placed at an extreme angle. Tinted glass is standard.

These are non-functional rear scoops and appear on the SportsRoof and Mach 1; are not used on the Hardtops and Convertibles.

The rear window of the Hardtop is more erect than on the SportsRoof. Convertible rear window is again standard in vinyl but the folding glass rear window remains as an available option. Vinyl roof seen here is an option available in black or parchment.

Distinctive rear-facing quarter panel exhaust trim is standard on Hardtops and Convertibles.

Rear windows of the SportsRoof model pivot open. Those on the Hardtop and Convertible models are cranked down (see page 227).

New SportsRoof body has smooth lines from roof to rear end.

Hardtop and Convertible have relatively flat rear deck lid.

Rear side reflector takes on a new shape for 1969, replacing rectangular units of 1968 (page 195).

Built-in rear spoiler adds to appearance of SportsRoof.

New tail lights replace 1968 style (page 195).

1969

Again in 1969, an Interior Decor Group was offered providing deluxe seat trim, courtesy lights in the doors, molded door trim panels with integral arm rests, a 3-spoke Rim-Blow steering wheel and a remote control outside rear view mirror. In addition, a Deluxe Interior Decor Group provided all of this plus teak-toned instrument panel appliques and an electric clock! Views of this deluxe interior will be found on pages 243 and 244.

Standard door panel

This Mustang emblem is used on the standard door panels only.

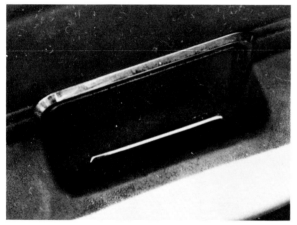

Concealed door latch release is reached through the arm rest.

Window crank handles are secured with machine screw concealed by a disposable vinyl trim disc.

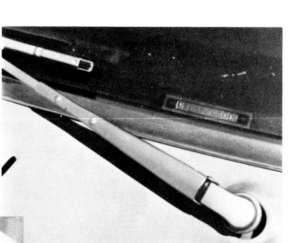

In 1969, a data plate was placed on the left front door (left), and the VIN number was *also* affixed to the left side of the instrument panel just behind the Windshield.

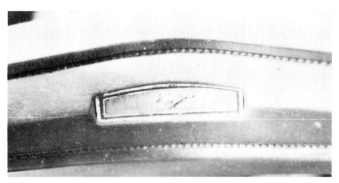

A new emblem appears at the hub of the 1969 standard steering wheel.

The standard steering wheel is a two-spoke energy-absorbing unit mounted on a cushioned steering column.

The standard rear seat of the SportsRoof and Mach 1 does not fold, but this feature is available as an extra-cost Option.

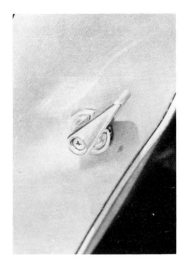

Front seat backs have a latching mechanism.

Hardtop and Convertible front seats have adjustable head rests; Mach 1 has high-backed seats with integral rests. See page 244 for view of these seats which are optional in other models.

Standard instruments include Alternator (left) 120 MPH Speedometer (left, below), combination Fuel and Temperature instrument (below right), and Oil Pressure gauge (right).

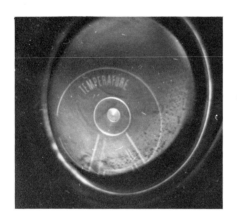

Optional instrumentation provides Temperature (left), special 140 MPH speedometer with odometer and integral reset (below left), 8000 RPM tachometer (with built-in OIL and ALT warning lights), and Fuel gauge (right).

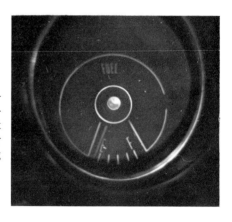

This is optional AM radio. Also available are AM/FM Stereo, and StereoSonic Tape/AM radio system with in-door speakers.

Standard heater/defroster control panel is placed just beneath the radio.

The optional SelectAire Conditioner has a distinctive control panel which replaces the standard unit, and cooling air outlets installed on the instrument panel (left and above).

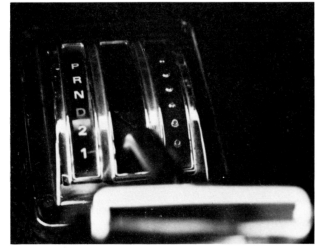

A new indicator plate (compare 1968 type on page 199) appears for 1969.

The standard built-in ash tray is located below the temperature control panel.

1969 MUSTANG GT

The GT Equipment Group was offered for the last time in 1969. Available with Hardtop, SportsRoof, or Convertible model, the Option added, in addition to a choice of five V-8 engines (from the 351 2V engine through the 428 Cobra Jet Ram Air engine; see Specifications), dual exhausts with quad outlets on the four bigger engines, styled steel wheels with wide-oval tires, stiffer suspension, quicker steering, pop-open GT gas cap, special stripes, and a hood with simulated air scoop, or, with a functional "shaker" scoop with the big 428 Cobra Jet Ram Air engine.

Standard quad-headlight system obviates need for GT-type fog lamps used earlier.

1969 MUSTANG GT SportsRoof　　　　　*Mr. Gerald Maly, Oceanside, California*

GT models have unique side stripes, but no other special ornamentation or trim.

A hood with decorative air scoop is supplied with the GT Equipment Group option. Optional Cobra Jet Ram-Air 428 V-8 engine is equipped with a functional (shaker) hood (page 234).

Built-in turn signal indicators are a feature of this hood.

Engine size is indicated by insignia on sides of the scoop.

Special GT pop-open gas cap is part of the GT Option.

Hood is locked with standard pin-type locks, not the turn-screw style used on the 1968 GT/CS.

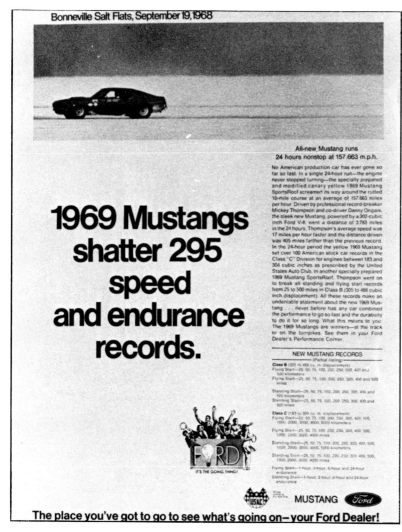

By late 1968, specially prepared Mustangs were setting various speed records to establish a reputation for the car as a Performance vehicle. In this advertisement a Canary Yellow 302 CID engined 1969 Mustang SportsRoof was reported to have run at an average of *over* 157 miles per hour for 24 hours, a total of 3,783 miles!

1969 MUSTANG BOSS 302

Based on the Trans-Am racing versions of the Mustang SportsRoof, the BOSS 302 uses a special version of the 302 CID engine. Specially designed cylinder heads feature canted valves and high-turbulence combustion chambers (now wedge shaped due to the canted valves). Pistons are extruded pop-up type raising compression to 11:1 against the standard 10.5:1. A new dual-point vacuum/centrifugal distributor, camshaft with solid lifters, forged crankshaft with 4-bolt main bearing caps, forged piston rods and a huge 780 CFM Holley Carburetor are all standard.

To protect the engine from accidental over-speed, a new Electronic RPM Limiter is provided. Connected into the ignition circuit, this ingenious device shorts out cylinders at random starting as the engine reaches 6150 RPM to limit its speed.

Mr. John Baum, Westminster, California

233

1969 BOSS 302

The "shaker air scoop" is mounted atop the carburetor intake and protrudes through a cut-out in the matching hood. Standard on the big Cobra Jet Ram-Air V-8, it is available as an Option for other models, including the BOSS 302.

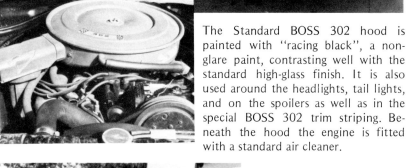

The Standard BOSS 302 hood is painted with "racing black", a non-glare paint, contrasting well with the standard high-glass finish. It is also used around the headlights, tail lights, and on the spoilers as well as in the special BOSS 302 trim striping. Beneath the hood the engine is fitted with a standard air cleaner.

The BOSS 302 has a standard front spoiler which extends below the lower valence panel. Its purpose is to add turbulence to the air passing below the car and thus reduce lift and drag.

Dual racing mirrors are an Option, but are mandatory with Sports Slats option (next page).

The BOSS 302 has no rear quarter air scoop as does the standard SportsRoof model (page 221) on which it is based.

BOSS 302 features standard "MAGNUM 500" deep dish 15" wheels in Argent with bright chrome trim rings. Wheels have wide 7" rim and standard F60 x 15 Super Wide Oval tires are used in the unique flared-fender wheel wells.

1969 BOSS 302

An optional Rear Spoiler, like the one in front, is aerodynamically designed, and exerts a downward force on the rear of the vehicle.

The rear-window Sports Slats Option provides interior shade for rear seat passengers. Releasing a spring-loaded catch (left) allows hinged assembly to be raised (right) for cleaning glass.

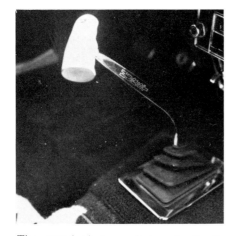

The standard transmission is Ford's close-ratio manual 4-speed, and an optional gear set is available for even quicker acceleration. Late in 1969, the Hurst Competition Shifter replaced standard Ford linkage in BOSS 302.

BOSS 302 V-8

COBRA JET Ram-Air V-8

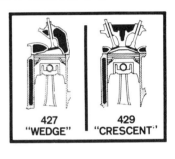

427 "WEDGE"   429 "CRESCENT"

Late in 1969, the BOSS 429 was offered for those wanting the "ultimate Muscle Car". Featuring the powerful 429 engine, rated at over 370 horsepower, the BOSS 429 was the only Mustang ever to use this.

New Aluminum heads with extremely large, round, free-flowing ports, a high rise intake manifold, and contoured exhaust manifolds were an important part of the BOSS 429 engine's features. The heads contained over-sized valves set at an angle so that the intakes were closer to that manifold and the exhausts closer to the exhaust manifold with a resulting crescent-shaped combustion chamber. Carburetor is a 735 CFM Holley with a manually-controlled air intake. Other features of the BOSS 429 including both Standard and Mandatory Options are:

Boss 429 CID V-8 Engine
High-Capacity Engine Oil Cooler
65 Ampere Alternator
85 Ampere Battery (mounted in trunk)
Power Steering with Oil Cooler
Magnum 500 15 x 7 Chrome-plated wheels
Tachometer
Interior Decor Group
Console
Dual-Point Dual-Advance Distributor

Power Front Disc Brakes
"Traction-Lok" Rear Axle
High-Performance Suspension
Front Spoiler
F60 x 15 Super Wide Oval tires
Dual Racing Mirrors
High-Back Bucket Seats
Visibility Group
Deluxe Seat Belts

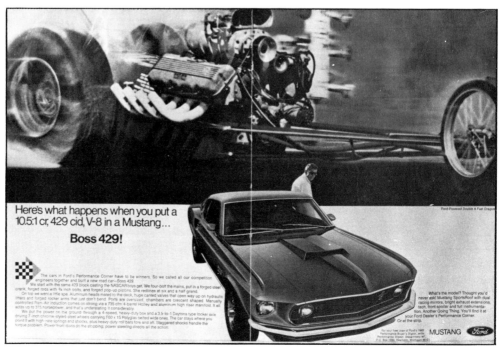

1969 SHELBY GT 350

The end of the line was approaching for the GT 350/500 as it varied less and less from available standard Mustang Options. Ford's recently introduced BOSS 302 and BOSS 429 were even more Performance-oriented, and less interest remained in continuing the Shelby cars as psuedo-competitors to those cars. Increasing legislative restrictions added to the practical limitations of offering what amounted to two differing, yet similar, models, and after the 1969 Model Year, production of the Shelbys was to be terminated. Although some few left-over 1969 cars were to be given cosmetic change and offered as 1970 models, for all practical purposes, production of these fine machines ended here.

Mr. Sam Telleson, La Mesa, California

Specifications

Engines

	GT 350 Ram-Air 351	GT 350 Base 302	GT 500 Ram-Air 428
Bore x stroke	4.00 x 3.50	4.002 x 3.00	4.13 x 3.98
Displacement	351 Cu. In.	302 Cu. In.	428 Cu. In.
Comp. ratio	10.7 to 1	9.0 to 1	10.6 to 1
Carb. type	Autolite 4V		Holley 4V
bhp @ rpm	290 @ 4800	220 @ 4600	335 @ 3200 (Est.)
Torque @ rpm	385 @ 3400	300 @ 2600	440 @ 3400 (Est.)

Drive Train

Clutch: 11-in. single disc. (11.5-in. on GT 500.)

Transmission: Ford four-speed, fully synchronized. (Optional on GT 350, close-ratio four-speed standard on GT 500.) Ford SelectShift Cruise-O-Matic three-speed, optional.

Brakes: Power assisted floating caliper 11.3-in. front discs with dual master cylinder and 10-in. x 2.0-in. rear drums with high performance linings. Swept area 232 sq. in.

Wheels: 15 x 7.0-in. composite design.

Tires: Goodyear belted E 70 x 15 Wide Oval.

Power, linkage type with belt driven pump. Recirculating ball and nut steering gear.

Suspension: Front—independent with coil springs above upper arm. Heavy duty adjustable shock absorbers with special valving. Heavy duty front stabilizer bar. Rear—Hotchkiss drive with variable rate semi-elliptic leaf springs and heavy duty adjustable shock absorbers with special valving.

General

	SportsRoof	Convertible
Curb weight (Est.)	3,600 lbs.*	3,689 lbs.‡
Weight dist. (Est.)	55/45**	54/46‡‡
Wheelbase	108.0 in.	108.0 in.
Track		
Front	58.5 in.	58.5 in.
Rear	58.5 in.	58.5 in.
Length	190.62 in.	190.62 in.
Height	50.6 in.	51.5 in.
Body/frame type	Welded steel unitized	Welded steel unitized

SportsRoof models have integral padded steel roll bar; quick detach inertia reel double shoulder harness with deluxe belts. Convertibles have styled padded roll bar and inertia reel single cross-chest shoulder harness with deluxe belts.

(*3,850 lbs. on GT 500), (‡ 3,939 lbs. on GT 500), (**57/43 on GT 500), (‡‡ 58/42 on GT 500)

Options:

☐ SelectShift Cruise-O-Matic automatic 3-speed ☐ Close-ratio 4-speed transmission Std. GT 500—Opt. GT 350 ☐ Heavy-duty battery Std. GT 500—Opt. GT 350 ☐ Traction-Lok available with GT 350/500 (except with air-conditioning) ☐ Fold-down rear seat available with GT 350/500 (SportsRoof only) ☐ Air-conditioning available on GT 500 with automatic transmission only. GT 350—all transmissions ☐ AM radio ☐ AM/FM Stereo radio ☐ AM Radio stereo tape system ☐ Forced ventilation available SportsRoof only ☐ Tinted glass ☐ Intermittent windshield wiper ☐ Tilt-away steering wheel ☐ F60 x 15 super low profile Goodyear Polyglas belted tires

1969 SHELBY GT 350/500

The 1969 Shelby GT 350/500 front fenders are all-fiberglass (as is the hood and the rear deck lid), and extend the overall length almost 3¼ inches over the standard SportsRoof or Convertible.

The 1969 Shelby GT 350 and GT 500 use a single pair of headlamps in place of the Mustang's dual quad lights, but do have auxiliary driving lights (below).

Unique parking lights and imported Lucas driving lights appear below the bumper.

A chromed trim strip is placed on the hood lip and front fenders to match the appearance of the bumper.

Fiberglass hood has built-in duct matching air intake to carburetor air cleaner (right).

The fiberglass hood and front fenders extend the front end by over three inches. Note functional front fender air scoops.

Recessed hood locks are secured by these brackets.

Functional hood scoops have expanded-metal protective grills.

1969 SHELBY GT 350/500

Again, functional air scoops are placed on rear quarter panels.

Shelby insignia replaces Mustang emblem on the SportsRoof roof quarter panel (page 224), but appears on the front fenders of the Convertible.

The license plate is relocated and hinged to allow access to fuel tank. Sequential turn signals are identical to 1965 Thunderbird.

A massive cast aluminum dual exhaust outlet now appears in former license plate location.

All 1969 GT 350/500 vehicles were assembled with the Deluxe Interior Decor Group trim as standard equipment. This same interior was an extra-cost Option on regular Mustang production cars.

Deluxe inside door panels have molded-in arm rests and are carpeted at the bottom.

Optional Remote-Control Left-Hand Outside Mirror has recessed control knob on deluxe molded door panels.

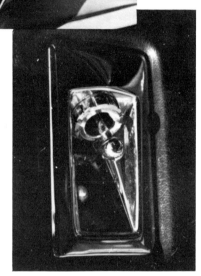

Shelby insignia appears on door panels of GT 350/500.

In addition to the Special Performance Vehicle Ford data plate, a Shelby Automotive plate appears on the left door.

Door hardware is same as standard interior.

High-backed bucket seats are standard in the GT 350/500 and the Mach 1 for 1969, and are Options in other models.

The Cobra GT 350 (or GT 500) emblem appears on the right side of the instrument panel.

Curved side window glass continues, but starting in 1968 the surrounding bright metal frame was omitted.

The deluxe 3-spoke Rim-Blow steering wheel is part of the Interior Decor Group Option, standard in the GT 350/500.

The 140 MPH speedometer with resettable trip odometer is standard.

A matching 8000 tachometer is again supplied.

Reminder lights are supplied for the seat belts and parking brake.

Gauges are again added for the Oil Pressure and charging functions, deleted with the installation of the tachometer.

A console is standard in the GT 350/500 and Mach 1, optional in others. Switches in the GT 350/500 control interior lighting and the Lucas fog lights.

The Shelby GT 350/500 cars were to be discontinued in 1970, and the COBRA name applied to a Torino-based SportsRoof, but Mustang's muscle cars, the BOSS 302 and MACH 1 continued to lead the pack.

Your Guide to the Winning Fords

BOSS 302

Trans-Am Triumphs:
- Michigan International
- Lime Rock
- Bridgehampton
- Donnybrooke

Setting up Mustangs for two Trans-Am championships showed us how to build Boss 302 for the road. It goes quick, hangs tight and stops quicker. Standard specs read like a $9000 European sports job instead of a reasonably priced, reliable American Pony car. Boss 302—one for the road.

FORD Ford

TORINO COBRA

Cobra's a whole new thing for '70. That SportsRoof shape is as good as it looks. We proved it in our own wind tunnel. It's a top-gun muscle car with no frills that puts 429 cu. in. of stocker in your driveway for very little money; 360 horsepower is standard. So is competition suspension and 4-speed box. With Hurst® Shifter. Cobra—this one's for real!

Grand National Wins:
- Riverside
- Daytona 500
- Carolina 500
- Firecracker 400
- Virginia 500
- Yankee 600
- Dixie 500
- Southern 500

MACH 1

The name that echoed like a bellowing exhaust note at Bonneville, when Mickey Thompson broke 295 records in his specially modified Mach I. '70 Mach I power begins with a 351 V-8 and goes up to a 428 Cobra Jet Ram-Air V-8. The only thing cool about Mach I is its looks.

Bonneville Records*:
Set by Mickey Thompson in Sept., 1968
(Class B—305 to 488 CID)
- Flying Start—
  25 to 500 km.
  25 to 500 miles
- Standing Start—
  25 to 500 km.
  25 to 500 miles

*partial listing only

Continuing the familiar theme "Mustang's the car designed to be designed by you", the 1970 model was offered as "Hot, Cool, Quick, Slick, or Rich". With bright new "Grabber" colors and interiors featuring upbeat stripes and houndstooth checks, a new oval steering wheel (to ease entrance and exit), a locking steering column, standard front and rear side marker lights that flash with the turn signals, standard high-backed bucket seats in all models, and a new 351 CID engine option, styling and design changes made the 1970 model the . . . "Mustang That's Got Personality".

facts on number one!

SPECIFICATIONS:

Color and Trim: 16 brilliant Super Diamond Lustre Enamel exterior finishes, and 6 standard vinyl interior trims, 6 knitted vinyl trims in Mach 1, 5 cloth and vinyl trims in Grandé. Also 2 Blazer cloth and 4 knitted vinyl trims in Decor Group.

ENGINES:

200 CID 1V Six—120 hp; 3.68" bore x 3.13" stroke; 8.8 to 1 comp. ratio; 7 main bearings; reg. fuel.

250 CID 1V Six—155 hp; 3.68" bore x 3.91" stroke; 9.0 to 1 comp. ratio; 7 main bearings; reg. fuel.

302 CID 2V V-8—220 hp; 4.00" bore x 3.00" stroke; 9.5 to 1 comp. ratio; regular fuel.

302 CID 4V "Boss" V-8—290 hp; 4.00" bore x 3.00" stroke; 10.6 to 1 comp. ratio; premium fuel.

351 CID 2V V-8—250 hp; 4.00" bore x 3.50" stroke; 9.5 to 1 comp. ratio; regular fuel.

351 CID 4V V-8—300 hp; 4.00" bore x 3.50" stroke; 11.0 to 1 comp. ratio; premium fuel.

428 CID 4V Cobra V-8*—335 hp; 4.13" bore x 3.98" stroke; 10.6 to 1 comp. ratio; premium fuel.

428 CID Cobra Jet Ram-Air 4V V-8*—335 hp; 4.13" bore x 3.98" stroke; 10.6 to 1 compression ratio; premium fuel.

429 CID 4V "Boss" V-8—375 hp; 4.36" bore x 3.60" stroke; 10.5 to 1 comp. ratio; premium fuel.

*Optional Drag Pack includes Traction-Lok differential with 3.91 axle ratio or "Detroit Locker" (No-Spin) differential with 4.30 axle ratio, plus these 428-cu. in. 4V engine modifications: engine oil cooler, cap screw connecting rods, modified crankshaft, flywheel and damper. Available with 428-cu. in. 4V non Ram-Air or Ram-Air V-8's.

Engine Features: 6000-mile (or 6-month) maintenance schedule with full-flow disposable type oil filter; dry element air cleaner; auto. choke; self adjusting valves with hydraulic lifters (mechanical valves, Boss 429); 12-volt electrical system; 42-amp. alternator, 45 amp-hr battery with 250 thru 351 CID engines, 55-amp. with automatic transmission on 200, 351 engines; 55-amp. alternator and 80 amp-hr battery with 428's, 429's.

TRANSMISSIONS:

3-Speed Manual: fully synchronized.

4-Speed Manual: sports-type w/Hurst Shifter.

SelectShift Cruise-O-Matic Drive: 3-speed fully automatic transmission which may be used manually to hold first or second gear for engine braking, better hill control hauling trailers.

MUSTANG POWER TEAMS

Engines	Transmissions			
	3-Speed Manual	Select-Shift	4-Speed Manual Wide-Ratio	4-Speed Manual Close-Ratio
200 Six (120 hp)	X	X		
250 Six (155 hp)	X	X		
302 V-8 (220 hp)	X	X	X	
302 Boss V-8 (290 hp)			X	X
351 V-8 2V (250 hp)	X	X	X	X
351 V-8 4V (300 hp)	X	X	X	X
428 V-8 Cobra (335 hp)		X		X
428 V-8 Cobra Jet (335 hp)		X		X
429 Boss V-8 (375 hp)				X

Rear Axle: semi-floating hypoid type; permanently lubricated rear wheel bearings.

Front Suspension: angle-poised ball-joint type with coil springs; strut-stabilized lower arms; link-type stabilizer.

Rear Suspension: asymmetrical variable-rate design longitudinal 4-leaf springs. Diagonally mounted shocks.

Steering: recirculating ball-type, permanently lubricated. 25.45 to 1 overall ratio (20.48 to 1 power). Turning diameter 37.6 ft.

Brakes: dual hydraulic system with dual master cylinder. Self-adjusting. self-energizing design. Lining areas: 130.4 sq. in. (200 Six); 154.0 sq. in. (250 Six, 302 V-8); 173.3 sq. in. (351, 428's); Boss 302, 232.0 sq. in. swept area.

Dimensions and Capacities: Length 187.4"; Width 71.7"; Height 51.5" (SportsRoof—50.6"); Wheelbase 108"; Track 58.5"; Trunk 8.3 cu. ft. (hardtop), 7.2 cu. ft. (SportsRoof). 7.2 cu. ft. (convertible). Fuel—20 gallons (in California, 22 gal. std.).

Weight: Hardtop—3080 lb.; SportsRoof—3104 lb.; Convertible—3190 lb.

STANDARD EQUIPMENT

Hardtop—Power Team: 200-cu. in. Big Six and fully synchronized 3-speed manual transmission • floor mounted shift lever • color-keyed loop-pile carpeting • courtesy lights • cigarette lighter • reversible keys • keyless locking • heater/defroster • all vinyl interior • curved side glass • high back bucket seats • locking steering column • Hurst Shifter (with 4-speed man. trans.) • Twice a-Year Maintenance • glove box • color-keyed headlining • printed circuit instrument panel • aluminized and stainless steel muffler • E78-14 belted bias-ply BSW tires. Plus all FORD MOTOR COMPANY LIFEGUARD DESIGN SAFETY FEATURES.

Mustang Grandé— In addition to the features listed for Hardtop: special sound insulating package • luxury cloth and vinyl seat trim • molded door trim panels and courtesy lights • deluxe 2-spoke steering wheel • woodtone instrument panel appliques • electric clock • bright floor pedal trim • dual color-keyed racing mirrors including remote-control LH mirror • dual bodyside paint stripe • black or white "Landau" vinyl roof covering • houndstooth check interior trim fabrics in 5 colors • glove compartment lock, wheel covers • rocker panel molding with vinyl insert • lower back panel applique • wheel lip molding

Convertible — In addition to features listed for Hardtop: 5-ply power-operated vinyl top • glass backlite • color keyed boot • easy-action top fastening latches • full width rear seat • courtesy lights under instrument panel.

SportsRoof— In addition to Hardtop features: integral rear deck spoiler • swing-out rear quarter windows • tinted glass backlite • courtesy lights under instrument panel, rear compartment.

Mustang Mach 1— In addition to Hardtop features listed previously: Power Team: 351-cu. in. 2V V-8 and fully synchronized 3-speed manual transmission • non-functional hood scoop/integral turn signal indicators • competition suspension • outside color-keyed dual racing mirrors • knitted vinyl high-back bucket seats/accent stripes • console with woodtone applique • Rim-Blow deluxe

three-spoke steering wheel • bright dual exhaust extensions • hood lock pins • Honeycomb back panel applique • wide-oval belted WSW tires • pop-open gas cap • dark argent extruded aluminum rocker panel molding • deck lid tape stripe (die-cast "Mach 1") • black painted hood and tape engine numerals (white painted hood and tape engine numerals available w/black or dark green) • die-cast center deep dish sports wheel covers • sport lamps in grille • woodtone cluster with right-hand instrument panel applique • electric clock • bright pedal pads • molded door trim panels w/courtesy lights • NVH sound package • carpet runners.

Mustang Boss 302: In addition to Hardtop and SportsRoof features listed above: Power Team: 302-cu. in. 4V V-8 engine rated at 290 hp and 4-speed manual transmission equipped with Hurst Shifter • black taillamp bezels • black chrome backlite molding and black headlamp castings • color-keyed dual racing mirrors • black hood and rear deck lid and black lower back panel • F60-15 belted BSW tires w/white letters • hub cap/trim ring • space saver spare • bodyside/hood stripes • Boss 302 tape identification on front fender (black only) • dual exhausts • quick ratio steering (16:1) • competition suspension including staggered rear shocks • special cooling package • 3.50 non-locking axle • front spoiler • 45 ampere battery • power front disc brakes.

Every 1970 Mustang includes these Ford Motor Company Lifeguard Design Safety Features: Dual hydraulic brake system with warning light • Glare reduced instrument panel padding, windshield wiper arms, steering wheel hub, rearview mirror/mirror mounting and windshield pillars • Energy-absorbing steering column, steering wheel, arm-rests and safety-designed door handles • Front and rear lap belts • Shoulder belts for front outboard occupants (except convertibles) • Turn indicators with lane-changing signal feature • Inside yield away rearview mirror • Energy-absorbing instrument panel with padding • Padded sun visors • Two-speed windshield wipers • Windshield washers • High strength laminate safety glass windshield • Double-yoke safety door latches and safety hinges • Emergency flasher • Backup lights • Side marker lights • Energy-absorbing front seat back tops with padding • Self-locking front seat backs • Safety-designed radio control knobs and push buttons • Outside rearview mirror, driver's side • Safety rim wheel and load-rated tires • Corrosion-resistant brake lines • Uniform transmission shift quadrant • Parking lamps coupled with headlamps • Non-reversing odometer • Safety design front end structure • High-back seats • Safety glove box latch.

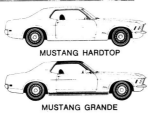

MUSTANG HARDTOP

MUSTANG GRANDE

MUSTANG SPORTSROOF

MUSTANG MACH 1

MUSTANG CONVERTIBLE

MUSTANG BOSS 302

1970 MUSTANG GRANDE

Mr. Donald Geiger, Fallbrook, California

1970 MUSTANG Convertible

New 351 CID engine had special added side emblem.

Mr. Bruce Forinash, Oceanside, California

A single pair of headlights replaces the four lamps used in 1969. Electrically not interchangeable, they are also spaced somewhat further apart than the inner pair of 1969 lamps.

The grill emblem, although same as 1968, is now placed at the center instead of offset. The grill pattern is changed to larger rectangles (page 222).

A redesigned front fender cap conceals the location of the former outer pair of headlamps with an interesting new simulated air scoop (right).

Parking lights continue to be protected beneath the bumper.

New side marker lights are now placed high on fender sides, and together with the new rear lamps (page 252) also operate simultaneously with the turn signals for added effect.

The MUSTANG GRANDE, introduced in 1970, is a version of the Hardtop which includes several deluxe features as standard. Among these are a special sound-insulating package, the Interior Decor Group, an electric clock, special houndstooth check upholstery, and a black or white vinyl covered roof, generally done "landau" style, with only the front _half_ covered.

Grande script appears on roof quarters.

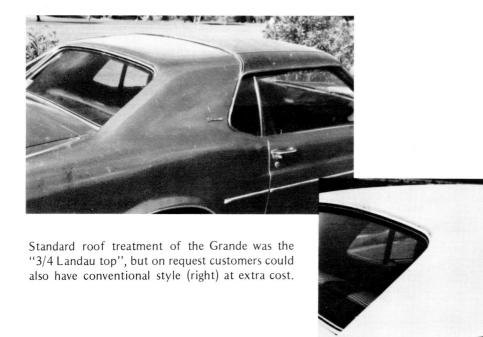

Standard roof treatment of the Grande was the "3/4 Landau top", but on request customers could also have conventional style (right) at extra cost.

The body side paint stripe is standard on the Grande model as is the rocker panel molding with a vinyl insert.

251

The black lower back panel applique is a standard feature on the Mustang Grande and BOSS 302 only.

Tail lamps are now recessed, rather than protruding as in 1969 (page 225).

New rear marker lamps (not reflectors as previously) also operate simultaneously with turn signals.

The left-side remote operated mirror is standard on the Grande, Mach 1, and the BOSS 302 models.

Backup lamps are standard on all models.

Grande interior features special houndstooth check trim patterns.

Mustang emblem appears on molded door panel.

Molded door panel is part of Interior Decor Group luxury trim Option.

Courtesy lamps are built into molded door panel below arm rest.

Front seatbacks are latched, but release is moved to bottom of seat (compare page 244).

In 1970, the Interior Decor Group Option includes choice of knitted vinyl, or new blazer-striped seat inserts.

Standard interiors also have high-backed bucket seats.

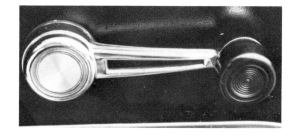

A new locking steering column sees the ignition switch moved up under the steering wheel.

A two-spoke steering wheel (deluxe version shown) is standard for 1970. A 3-spoke Rim-Blow (standard in Mach 1) is again an available Option.

Round electric clock (left) on right side of panel is standard in the Grande, an Option in Mach 1. Alternately, a rectangular electric clock is an Option in other models.

Grande emblem appears on instrument panel (right).

Interior of Grande shows standard features, available as part of optional Interior Decor Group in other models, including wood-toned appliques on the instrument panel.

1970 instruments resemble those used in 1969, but speedometers differ. An inner scale of metric numbers has been added to the speedometer (lower left) used exclusively on the Grande; others use the unit shown on page 261.

An AM/FM Stereo radio, provided with in-door speakers (below), is another Option.

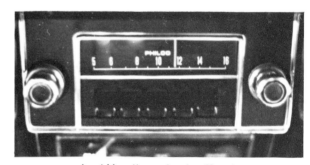

An AM radio option is offered.

A third Option, the Stereo-Sonic Tape/AM Radio System also plays through speakers in the doors.

1970 BOSS 302

1970 BOSS 302

'70 Boss 302-Son of Trans-Am.

The Mustang Boss 302 is what comes from winning those Trans-Am championships. From its 5-litre, F.I.A. sanctioned V-8 to its 16-to-1 steering, the Boss is designed to go quick and hang tight. The standard specs sound like a $9,000 European sports job instead of a reasonably priced, reliable American pony car. Boss 302 comes in just one body style—the wind-splitting Sports-Roof shape. The engine

is Ford's high output 302 CID 4V V-8, with new cylinder heads to permit canting the valves for better gas flow and larger diameter—2.18" intake, 1.71" exhaust. That's what gives you a big 290 horsepower from a small, lightweight 302 CID engine.

Choose either close or wide ratios on Boss 302's buttersmooth, fully synchronized 4-speed. We've made it an even quicker box by adding a T-Handle Hurst Shifter.❋ Brakes are power boosted, ventilated floating-caliper

front discs. When we tell you the suspension is competition type with staggered rear shocks to combat rear wheel hop on takeoff, don't take our word for it, give it a try. We glue the Boss to the road on 15-inch wheels with hub cap trim rings, shod with F60x15 superwide fiberglass belted bias-ply tires. All this standard equipment leaves you little to option but the fun things—like Magnum 500 chrome wheels, and those great Sport Slats for the tinted back-lite. That's Boss 302. Your only problem . . . deciding whether to drive it or "Trans-Am" it.

Car and Driver Magazine says, "The Boss 302 . . . may just be the new standard by which everything from Detroit must be judged."

Two Trans-Am Championships for Mustang taught us how to set up Boss 302.

MUSTANG *Ford*

These two pages tell you all about the 1970 Boss 302. They are part of Ford's 16-page '70 Performance Buyer's Digest. It includes detailed specifications and options on all the great 1970 performance Fords . . . Cobra, Torino GT, Boss 302, and Mach 1. There are also sections on Ford performance fun vehicles and Ford Muscle Parts. The Digest wraps it all up for you. For a copy just write to:

FORD PERFORMANCE DIGEST, Dept. RT-2
Box 747, Dearborn, Michigan 48121

Paint a number on your Boss 302, put a big gas tank in it, and call yourself Parnelli Jones.

With the same styling changes of the other models, the two Mustang Performance Cars, BOSS 302 and BOSS 429 continued to be manufactured in 1970, although both were of limited production and together accounted for only a small percentage of production. Outwardly quite similar, the BOSS 302 featured a High-Output version of the 302 engine with an announced rating of only 290 horsepower, a figure it easily exceeded. The BOSS 429 continued to offer the 375 horsepower "Crescent" engine with its mechanical lifters and high-compression canted-valve heads (page 237).

Mr. & Mrs. Ray Higuera, Escondido, California

257

The "Shaker" Hood Scoop is an optional accessory with the BOSS 302, or the 351 CID engines, but standard with the 428 CID Cobra Jet Ram-Air V-8.

The standard 1970 BOSS 302 hood has new distinctive painted striping (compare page 234).

The 1970 side striping also differs from 1969 (page 235), and the logo is now placed at the top of the fender.

The two BOSS models are supplied with standard 15" wheels, all others are mounted on 14" diameter wheels. Magnum 500 chrome wheels are an option, but four F60 x 15" wide oval tires are standard, and a "Space-Saver" tire (page 129) is provided for the spare.

The front air spoiler is standard, mounted below the regular lower front valence panel.

Dual racing mirrors are standard on the BOSS cars. The left side is remote-operated.

The quarter windows pivot open.

The NASCAR-style BOSS 429 engine with an optional dress-up kit including exhaust headers.

Commencing in 1969, the customary data plate was omitted from the left door. A decal sticker replaced it, and the Vehicle Identification Number was now stamped into the windshield.

A "tire size and recommended inflation pressure" decal is now placed on the right side door jamb.

The Sport Slats are an Optional accessory.

A BOSS feature is the black rear deck lid and lower back panel.

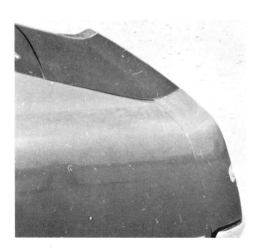

The standard built-in rear spoiler of the SportsRoof model suffices for the BOSS cars; external "functional" type (page 236) is an accessory.

The recessed tail lights feature a black-painted bezel on BOSS cars, rather than the bright trim of the other models (page 252).

A standard 1970 Speedometer is used in the BOSS cars.

A matching 8000 RPM Tachometer replaces the 2-function standard instrument (page 255) in BOSS cars.

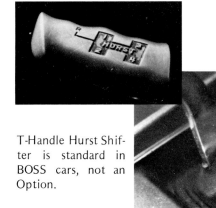

T-Handle Hurst Shifter is standard in BOSS cars, not an Option.

Standard high-backed bucket seats and interior are furnished, and the Console, optional in some other models, is standard for the BOSS.

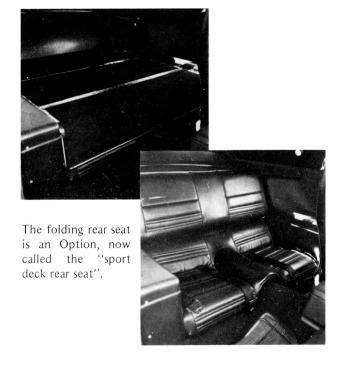

The folding rear seat is an Option, now called the "sport deck rear seat".

Mustang. It's a personal thing.

It happens every time. Get into a Mustang and something gets into you.

Is it because Mustang has more rooflines than all its competitors? A choice of seven different engines?

Or, for example, is it Mustang's new low-priced, lightweight 351 CJ V-8 that gives you high performance on regular gas?

Or is it because Mustang offers so many options to select from—so many ways to make it *your* car?

Is it the proud new profile of this Mach I? Is it the NASA-type hood scoops and competition suspension you get at no extra cost?

No. Mustang is more. It's greater than the sum of its parts. It's something you have to discover. Your Ford Dealer will help you.

Ford gives you better ideas. (A better idea for safety: Buckle up.)

262

Introduced late in August of 1970, the new 1971 Mustang offered a completely new look. Over two inches longer than the 1970 model, new long hoods featuring concealed windshield wipers joined with a thinner roof section and flush door handles to present obviously identifiable new features. New Options included a Special Instrumentation Group, a Rear Window Electric Defrost with conductive strips placed directly in the glass, and a Protection Group featuring body-side molding with color-keyed vinyl inserts and front bumper guards with rubber inserts as well as a vinyl roof covering for the SportsRoof model.

In the Performance area, a new BOSS 351 replaced the earlier BOSS 302. Featuring a new high-performance version of the 351 4V Cleveland engine not available on other models, the BOSS 351 powerplant generates 330 horsepower, has a compression ratio of 11.0:1, and uses a new Ford 750 CFM carburetor.

Mustang Specifications

Color and Trim: 16 Super Diamond Lustre Enamel exterior finishes (11 on Mach 1, Boss 351); 6 standard vinyl interior colors (5 in convertible); 6 knitted vinyl colors in Mach 1 Sports Interior Option and Convertible; 5 cloth/vinyl trims in Grandé; 2 knitted vinyl and 4 cloth/vinyl trims in Decor Group.

Engines*:

250 CID 1V Six—145 hp; 3.68" bore x 3.91" stroke; 9.0 to 1 comp. ratio; 7 main bearings; regular fuel.

302 CID 2V V-8—210 hp; 4.00" bore x 3.00" stroke; 9.0 to 1 comp. ratio; regular fuel.

351 CID 2V V-8—240 hp; 4.00" bore x 3.50" stroke; 9.0 to 1 comp. ratio; regular fuel.

351 CID 4V V-8—285 hp; 4.00" bore x 3.50" stroke; 10.7 to 1 comp. ratio; premium fuel.

351 CID 4V H.O. (Dual Ram Induction) V-8—330 hp; 4.00" bore x 3.00" stroke; 11.7 to 1 comp. ratio; premium fuel.

429 CID 4V CJ V-8—370 hp; 4.13" bore x 3.98" stroke; 11.3 to 1 comp. ratio; premium fuel.

429 CID 4V CJ-R (Dual Ram Induction) V-8—370 hp; 4.13" bore x 3.98" stroke; 11.3 to 1 comp. ratio; premium fuel.

*Hp ratings are gross hp derived from dynamometer.
**375 hp with Drag Pack option. Details page 15.

ENGINES	TRANSMISSIONS			
	3-speed Floor-Mounted Manual	Select-Shift	4-speed Manual Wide-Ratio	4-speed Manual Close-Ratio
250 Six (145 hp)	X	X		
302 V-8 (210 hp)	X	X		
351 V-8 (240 hp)	X	X		
351 V-8 (285 hp)			X	X
351 H.O. (330 hp)				X
429 CJ V-8 (370 hp)		X		X
429 CJ-R (370 hp)		X		X

Engine Features: 6000-mile (or 6-month) maintenance schedule with full-flow disposable type oil filter; dry element air cleaner; auto. choke; self-adjusting valves with hydraulic lifters (mechanical lifters on Boss 351 and with Drag Pack Option); 12-volt electrical system; 38-amp. alternator with 250 Six, 42-amp. with 302 & 351 V-8's, 55-amp. with 429 & Boss 351 V-8's; 45 amp-hr battery with 250 Six and 302 & 351 2V V-8's, 55 amp-hr with 351 4V V-8, 80 amp-hr with Boss 351 & 429 V-8's.

MODEL	STANDARD ENGINES	OPTIONAL V-8's
Hardtop, SportsRoof, Grandé, Convertible	250 1V Six (145 hp)	302 2V (210 hp) 351 2V (240 hp) 351 4V (285 hp) 429 4V CJ (370 hp**) 429 4V CJ-R (370 hp**)
Mach 1	302 2V V-8 (210 hp)	351 2V (240 hp) 351 4V (285 hp) 429 4V CJ (370 hp**) 429 4V CJ-R (370 hp**)
Boss 351	351 H.O. 4V V-8 (330 hp)	No optional engines available

Rear Axle: semi-floating hypoid type; permanently lubricated rear wheel bearings.

Front Suspension: angle-poised ball-joint type with coil springs; strut-stabilized lower arms; link-type stabilizer.

Rear Suspension: asymmetrical variable-rate design longitudinal 4-leaf springs. Diagonally mounted shocks.

Steering: recirculating ball-type, permanently lubricated. 27.7 to 1 overall ratio (22.1 to 1 power). Turning diameter 39.8 ft.

Brakes: dual hydraulic system with dual master cylinder. Self-adjusting, self-energizing design. Lining areas: 154.0 sq. in. (250 Six, 302 V-8); 173.3 sq. in. (351, 429); Boss 351, 231.0 sq. in. swept area.

Dimensions and Capacities: Length 189.5"; Width 74.1"; Height 50.8" (SportsRoof—50.1"; Convertible—50.5"); Wheelbase 109"; Track—rear 61.0", front 61.5"; Trunk 9.5 cu. ft. (Hardtop), 8.3 cu. ft. (SportsRoof), 8.1 cu. ft. (Convertible). Fuel—20 gallons.

Weight: Hardtop—3087 lb.; SportsRoof—3057 lb.; Convertible 3209 lb.

NOTE: Your new 1971 Mustang comes equipped with factory engineered and approved parts such as the dependable Autolite Sta-Ful battery, Autolite Power-Tip spark plugs, Autolite shock absorbers, and an Autolite 6000-mile oil filter. Be sure to specify genuine Autolite parts whenever replacement is necessary.

While the information shown herein was correct when approved for printing, Ford Division reserves the right to discontinue or change at any time, specifications or designs without incurring any obligation. Some features shown or described are optional at extra cost.

MUSTANG MACH 1

MUSTANG GRANDE

MUSTANG BOSS 351

MUSTANG HARDTOP

MUSTANG SPORTSROOF

MUSTANG CONVERTIBLE

1971 MUSTANG GRANDE

1971 MUSTANG HARDTOP

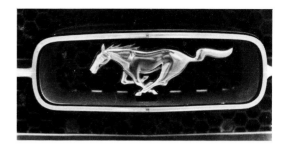

Mustang's "corral" returns for 1971.

Mr. Grady Stewart, Oceanside, California

New front end treatment for the Hardtop, the Grande and the Convertible finds the horizontal bars and Mustang "corral" returned to the grill. These are not used on the SportsRoof-based models (page 273).

The chromed trim strip across the hood lip and front fenders is a feature first seen on the 1969 Shelby GT 350/500 (page 240).

Mustang script introduced in 1969 coctinues to be used on the front fenders.

After using clear lenses on the parking lights from 1967 on, the new 1971 lens is again amber.

Rocker panel moldings and wheel opening moldings are standard on the Mustang Grande, options on the Hardtop and Convertible.

As previously, the hood is hinged at the rear and opens from the front.

The standard hood again has an embossed "windsplit", and new turned-up rear edge, adding to apparent length.

The windshield wipers are concealed beneath an upturned flare at the rear of the hood.

The inlet for the cowl air ventilators is a screened duct placed under the hood at the base of the windshield.

Grande script again appears on the roof quarters of that model.

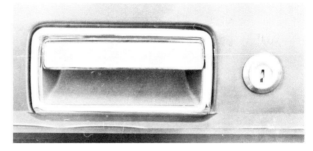

In a new styling feature, the vinyl roof covering of the Grande is recessed slightly from the window edges to add to the effect. The body side stripe seen here is a vinyl-filled trim strip included in the Protection Group Option along with rubber-faced front bumper guards.

A new flush-mounted recessed outside door handle, and its associated keylock, appears on the 1971 models replacing the familiar pushbutton handles used from the start of production.

A bold new triple-lens tail light assembly appears on all models for 1971.

Starting in 1971, the gas cap is no longer secured by a retaining wire (page 60).

The lower back panel, between the tail lights, on the Grande is covered with a black textured applique similar to that used on the Mach 1 and BOSS models.

New Lambeth cloth and Vinyl upholstery is color-coordinated with carpets and vinyl roof covering in the Grande; but the standard interior is all-vinyl. A Decor Group Option includes knitted vinyl inserts, and for Mach 1 there is a special Sports Interior Option with distinctive accent stripes.

Despite standard Grande console, there is room for two passengers in rear seat.

All models have High Back bucket seats and latching seatbacks with a latch handle at bottom rear (right). New for the year is an automatic seatback release operated by switches in the door jambs.

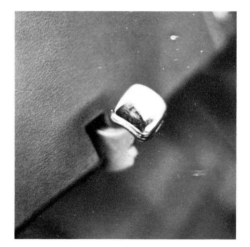

The window riser handles for 1970-72 models are the same, and a new option for 1971 is power-operated side windows.

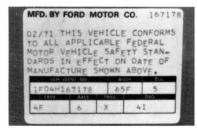

MFD. BY FORD MOTOR CO. 167178
02/71 THIS VEHICLE CONFORMS TO ALL APPLICABLE FEDERAL MOTOR VEHICLE SAFETY STANDARDS IN EFFECT ON DATE OF MANUFACTURE SHOWN ABOVE.

VEH. IDENT. NO.		BODY	COL.
1F04H167178		65F	5
TRIM	AXLE	TRANS	DSO
4F	6	X	41

The decal "data plate" appears again on the door edge.

This deluxe molded door panel is standard on the Grande, and a part of the Decor Group Option available on other models. Inside the door, a new Steel Guard Rail, standard on all 1971 models, is a box section door beam which helps absorb "side impact forces".

A re-styled instrument panel has hooded installations of speedometer, fuel gauge and four-function instruments (next page) placed deep in the instrument panel. This steering wheel is the optional Rim-Blow Deluxe 3-spoke wheel which allows the horn to be blown by pressing at any point on its circumference.

The standard steering wheel is a two-spoke unit with an attractive elongated Mustang emblem.

A round Mustang plastic emblem button appears at the hub of the optional Rim-Blow steering wheel.

This switch controls the new optional Rear Window Defogger. Pilot light at its left lights when system is ON; and standard warning lights to the right indicate seat BELTS and parking BRAKE functions.

A new Grande emblem appears on the 1971 instrument panel of that model replacing the script of 1970 (page 254).

Standard Fuel Gauge appears between speedometer and new 4-function matching instrument.

The standard speedometer, now located to the *right* of the matching instrument, is a 120 MPH unit which also has a metric scale. An optional similar unit is available with an integral trip odometer (page 275).

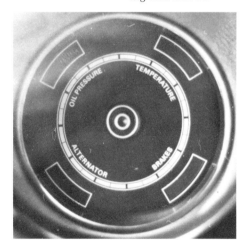

A new matching instrument indicated four functions including Oil Pressure, Temperature, Alternator, and a warning lamp to indicate a pressure loss in either side of the standard dual hydraulic brake system.

The SelectShift automatic transmission is an option on all but the BOSS cars which are available only with the manul 4-speed.

The fog lights are also standard on the Mach 1, but it does not have standard front spoiler.

The 1972 BOSS 351 was designed to replace the earlier BOSS 302, and was a Performance car built to handle the high-performance version of the "Cleveland" 351 CID engine introduced in 1970. The BOSS 351 engine was rated at 330 horse-power (at 5400 RPM), had a compression ratio of 11.0:1, and used a new Ford four-venturi carburetor with a capacity of 750 cubic feet per minute.

BOSS 351, like the earlier BOSS cars, had a competition-type suspension with heavy-duty front coil and rear left springs, heavier front stabilizer, and staggered rear shocks to reduce wheel hop at initial acceleration. Traction-Lok rear end was standard as was a manual 4-speed transmission with Hurst shift linkage.

Standard F60 x 15 tires were mounted on seven-inch rims, and wheel options included the attractive Magnum 500 wheels in either argent or chrome-plated finish. A space saver spare tire was standard as were Power Front Disc Brakes.

1971 BOSS 351

Special Interest Cars, Westminster, California

1971 BOSS 351

The standard BOSS 351 hood has black (or argent) paint treatment, and features NASA Scoops (below) which direct air through a built-in duct on the underside of the hood (below, right) where it is fed directly into the special carburetor intake. Standard on the BOSS 351 and the 429 Cobra Jet Ram-Air engines, it is also offered as an Option with the other two 351 CID V-8's.

New-style twist locks are standard on this hood.

Body side stripes are black or argent depending on body color. The BOSS 351 is available in 11 paint options including four new "Grabber" colors; lime, blue, green metallic, and yellow.

Normally the interior of the BOSS 351 is standard, but the Interior Decor Group was an available Option. A Hurst Competition Shifter was standard on the 4-speed transmission, and the Automatic Transmission was not offered for this model.

The otherwise optional Speedometer with Integral Trip Odometer is standard in the BOSS 351.

The Instrumentation Group, optional at extra cost on other models, is standard equipment on the BOSS 351. Gauges indicate Oil Pressure, Ampere Output, and Engine Temperature.

The lower back panel, and the lower valence panel, of the BOSS 351 have black or argent paint treatment, and the name is displayed on rear deck lid.

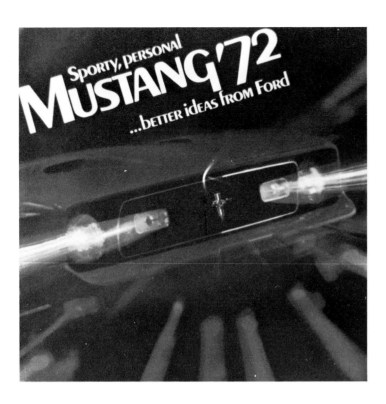

"Control and Balance Make It a Beautiful Experience"
announced the new 1972 advertisements. Whether you wished
to ski down a mountain or sail a boat in the water, the 1972
Mustangs were held to be for you. Designed to project the
rapidly diminishing "sporty" characteristics of the Mustang,
the ads emphasized good control and road handling.

New bodies had been introduced in 1971, and for 1972, changes would be almost exclusively cosmetic. An optional external Decor Group for the Hardtop and the Convertible added the sportlight-and-honeycomb-grill, replacing their standard 1971-style grill and emblem, but few other appearance changes were made.

The big change for 1972 was in the <u>elimination</u> of the Performance-oriented cars and options. Gone were the BOSS cars, and with them the big engines. The Cobra Jet 429 CID 370 horsepower V-8 of 1971 and its companion version, the Cobra Jet Ram-Air V-8 were no longer available. With all engines somewhat detuned, and burdened with new emission controls, horsepower was no longer mentioned. However, the engines <u>were</u> "cleaner". By Ford's estimate, "more than 85% of the hydrocarbon emissions, and nearly 70% of the carbon monoxide emissions are eliminated".

Mustang Hardtop

Mustang SportsRoof

Mustang Convertible

Mustang Mach I

Mustang Grandé

MUSTANG Ford

Ford gives you Better Ideas.

Mustang Specifications

Color and Trim: 16 Super Diamond Lustre Enamel exterior finishes (12 on Mach I and with Decor Group); 6 standard all-vinyl interior colors; 6 knitted vinyl colors in Convertible and in Mach I Sports Interior Option; 5 cloth and vinyl trims in Grandé; 5 vinyl roof colors. Check your local Ford Dealer for full details on color and trim availability.

ENGINES*

250 CID 1V Six—3.68" bore x 3.91" stroke; 7 main bearings; regular fuel.†

302 CID 2V V-8—4.00" bore x 3.00" stroke; regular fuel.†

351 CID 2V V-8—4.00" bore x 3.50" stroke; regular fuel.†

351 CID 4V V-8—4.00" bore x 3.50" stroke; regular fuel.†

*It is estimated that with all controls on the 1972 Mustang, more than 85% of hydrocarbon emissions and nearly 70% of carbon monoxide emissions are eliminated.

†All 1972 Mustang engines are designed to operate on regular gasoline with octane rating of at least 91 when the engine is adjusted to factory recommended specifications.

ENGINES	TRANSMISSIONS		
	3-Speed Floor-Mounted Manual	SelectShift	4-Speed Floor-Mounted Manual
250 1V Six	X	X	
302 2V V-8	X‡	X	
351 2V V-8	X‡	X	
351 4V V-8		X	X

NOTE: Availability of engines and transmissions is contingent upon Federal Emission Certification and production schedules.

‡Not available in California.

Engine Features: 6000-mile (or 6-month) maintenance schedule with full-flow disposable type oil filter; dry element air cleaner; automatic choke; self-adjusting valves with hydraulic lifters; 12-volt electrical system; 38-amp. alternator with 250 Six, 302 and 351 2V V-8's (42-amp. with 302 and 351 2V V-8's on Mach I), 55 amp. with 351 4V V-8; 45 amp-hr battery with 250 Six and 302 & 351 2V V-8's, 55 amp-hr with 351 4V V-8.

MODEL	STANDARD ENGINES	OPTIONAL V-8's
Hardtop, SportsRoof, Grandé, Convertible	250 1V Six	302 2V 351 2V 351 4V
Mach I	302 2V V-8	351 2V 351 4V

Rear Axle: semi-floating hypoid type; permanently lubricated rear wheel bearings.

Front Suspension: angle-poised ball-joint type with coil springs; strut-stabilized lower arms; link-type stabilizer.

Rear Suspensions: asymmetrical variable-rate design longitudinal 4-leaf springs. (Diagonally mounted shocks for 351 4V V-8 only.)

Steering: recirculating ball-type, permanently lubricated. 30.2 to 1 overall ratio (22.1 to 1 power). Turning diameter 39.8 feet.

Brakes: dual hydraulic system with dual master cylinder. Self-adjusting, self-energizing design. Lining areas: 163.6 sq. in. (250 Six, 302 V-8); 173.3 sq. in. (351 V-8's).

NOTE: Your 1972 Mustang comes with factory-engineered Autolite/Motorcraft battery, oil filter, shock absorbers, Autolite spark plugs and other Ford approved precision parts. For continued top performance, be sure to specify Autolite spark plugs and Autolite/Motorcraft parts whenever replacement is necessary.

NOTE: Information shown was correct when approved for printing. Ford Division reserves the right to discontinue, or change at any time, its product specifications or design without incurring obligations. Some items illustrated or described are optional at extra cost. Many options are offered on all models. Some are required in combination with other options. Always consult your Ford Dealer for complete details.

1972 MUSTANG HARDTOP

As part of an overall 1972 promotional effort, Ford offered a _new_ Spring Option for their Pintos, Mavericks, and Mustangs. Applicable either to the Mustang Sports Roof or Hardtop, the option included as "Package A", the following: Special Red, White and Blue exterior paint, Special USA shield on the rear fenders, an exterior Decor Group with color-keyed front bumper, accent tape stripes, accented back panel, trim rings and colored-keyed hub caps, racing mirrors, and a distinctive interior trim. In another group, "Package B" included all of the above plus raised-letter wide oval tires, competition suspension, and Magnum 500 Chrome Wheels in place of the trim rings and hub caps.

The 1972 Hardtop and Convertible were both furnished with the grill emblem and bars as standard equipment. A new Decor Group Option replaced these with the in-grill Sportlamps, front spoiler/bumper and color-keyed fender and hood-lip moldings (opposite page).

Hardtop and Convertible standard grill ornament.

Bright fender front molding is used with the standard grill treatment of Hardtop and Convertibles.

Beneath the optional front spoiler/bumper (standard on Sports Roof-based models), the recessed parking lamp is unchanged.

The standard front end treatment for the SportsRoof and the Mach 1 includes the integral spoiler/bumper and Sportslamp in the grill.

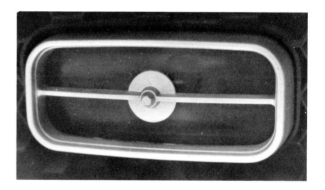

Sportslamps are right-and left-handed, to allow for grill curvature. Lens is amber, not clear.

The Mustang emblem appears on the grill center with Sportslamp installation.

Hood lip and fender front moldings are painted body color, not chromed as on Hardtop and Convertible (opposite page).

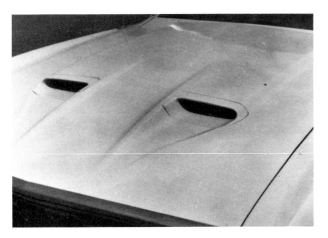

The standard 1972 hood is unchanged. It is used on all models including the Mach 1.

An Option with the 351 V-8 engines (also Mach 1 with base 302) is the Dual Ram Induction system which includes this hood with two functional NASA type air scoops. Incoming air is directed through ducts directly to the carburetor intake assembly.

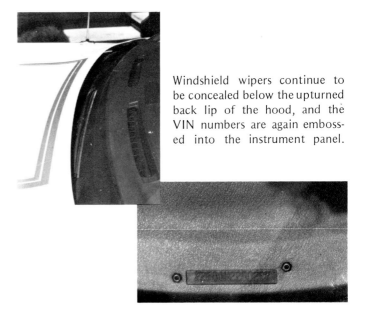

Windshield wipers continue to be concealed below the upturned back lip of the hood, and the VIN numbers are again embossed into the instrument panel.

Wheel lip and rocker panel moldings are standard on all models except the Mach 1.

Mustang script again appears on front fenders.

The distinctive rear roof line of the Hardtop conceals a recessed back window.

Script lettering replaces the M-U-S-T-A-N-G style used on the 1971 rear deck lid (page 268).

Most obvious change at the rear is the addition of the Mustang script above right tail light.

Rear lamp assembly is identical to 1971.

Two-spoke steering wheel is standard, but again a three-spoke Rim-Blow woodtoned Optional steering wheel is available.

From 1970 on, this "Safety Standards Certification Label" has been placed on the left front door, replacing the earlier metal data plate.

Standard door panel has separate arm rest assembly; Grande and optional Mach 1 Sports Interior have molded door panels.

Standard interiors are all-vinyl, and are used in all models except the Convertible (knitted vinyl), and the Grande which has Lambeth cloth and vinyl.

Latching high-back bucket seats are standard in all models.

Distinctive interior, upholstered in blue and white vinyl with red piping, is part of new Sprint Decor Option.

Control and balance make it a beautiful experience.

Most people look at waves and just see water. To them, a road's just pavement. But if you think there's more to life, we've got something for you.

Mustang's new Sprint Decor Option. Sporty colors inside and out. Dual racing mirrors that look right at home.

Even the interior of the Sprint Decor Option is a new experience. A panoramic instrument panel and a floor-mounted stick shift sitting between bucket seats. Now this is the real way to control a car.

Its stabilizer bar and independent front suspension help give you a more balanced ride. Around curves and over bumps.

The Sprint Decor Option is available in the Hardtop and SportsRoof models. Mag wheels, raised white letter tires and competition suspension are also available.

1972 Ford Mustang SportsRoof shown with Sprint Decor Option

FORD MUSTANG
FORD DIVISION

1972 Ford Mustang Hardtop shown with Sprint Decor Option.

"Control and Balance" advertising campaign (page 276) extends to new Sprint Decor Option.

Seat Belt Reminder light, an optional accessory, is installed on the instrument panel.

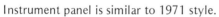

Instrument panel is similar to 1971 style.

Instruments are unchanged from 1971. Again a speedometer with an integral trip odometer was offered as an extra-cost Option.

In addition to the AM radio other options again include an AM/FM Stereo radio, and an AM radio with Stereosonic Tape System.

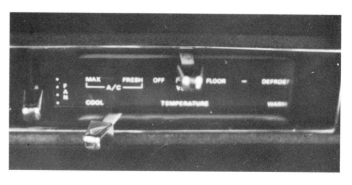

The optional SelectAire Conditioner control panel replaces standard heater/defroster panel.

mach 1
MUSTANG

In 1947, a now common expression, "Mach 1", was placed into our vocabulary when the "sound barrier" was broken for the first time as Captain Charles Yeager flew his rocket-powered X-1 aircraft faster than the speed of sound for the first time. Like many other expressions that had preceeded it, its origins are now unimportant for the automobile named for it will likely never exceed its original definition: "The Speed of Sound (approximately 743 miles per hour at sea level)".

The "original" Mach 1 was built by Ford's Design Center in Dearborn in 1967, but by 1968 a revised model, built as a racing-oriented experimental version of the 1968 Fastback 2+2 appeared. Strongly similar to the production car, it also resembled the Ford GT competition vehicles which were designed by the same group. Unique in many ways, several of its special design features were later to become production items including the quick-release gas cap, racing mirrors, deleted side vent windows, flared wheel openings, and air spoilers. An exciting-looking car, the Mustang Mach 1 was to be heavily publicized.

The name "Mach 1" was thus connected by Ford to a racing-type, sporty car intended for all-out road racing and driving, and when it first appeared on a version of the new 1969 SportsRoof, it was immediately accepted. Clearly a case of an excellent name selection and identification had again been made.

A top-of-the-line version of each year's new Mustang has been identified as the Mach 1 ever since. Although never the all-out muscle cars that the BOSS cars were in 1969-71, Mach 1, with its distinctive standard equipment and special bolt-on Options has always remained a distinctive and popular Driving Machine.

1972 MUSTANG Mach 1

Mr. Douglas Statser, Oceanside, California

The honeycomb black grill with integral sportlamps is standard on Mach 1.

The special dual intake hood is standard for Mach 1 but the plain hood (page 282) is an available choice with its standard 302 CID V-8 engine.

Black-painted or argent Bodyside tape stripes are a popular option and are also available on the Hardtops and Convertibles. Magnum 500 chrome wheels are optional, as are raised letter F70 x 14 tires.

Lower front valance panel on Mach 1 has black or argent paint treatment.

Lower side panel, beneath the Mach 1 identification, is painted black or argent (depending on body color).

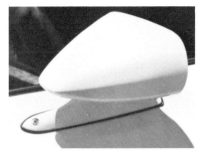

Color-keyed dual racing mirrors are standard.

Almost-flat rear window of the SportsRoof model blends with sloping roof line.

Rear quarter windows on Mach 1 do not open.

Mach 1 identification appears at center of deck lid just above key-lock.

Distinctive black honeycomb applique (right) is applied between tail lights.

By 1973, the Mustang had grown substantially (see chart below) and was no longer the small car that had excited the Market on its introduction in 1964. Almost ponderous, it had gained some 575 pounds, over twenty-two per cent of its introductory weight and was now over a foot longer. Aside from its rightful claim to a softer, safer, and more luxurious ride, it was now limited by applicable legislation. It could go no faster, further, or quicker, than the 1965 model as more powerful engines that had been a part of its progression had been withdrawn due to emission control and pollution limitation restrictions.

Thus, at the end of this model year, an entirely new Mustang would appear. So different that it was to bear a new designation (which conveniently overlooked early history of the marque), this new vehicle would be called the "MUSTANG II" and would mark the first successful attempt by a Detroit manufacturer to reduce the size and weight of a popular automobile. Mustang II would emerge as a "small car". Yet with its overall length of 175", curb weight of 2718 pounds, it was revealed as a car just a little shorter, and heavier, but otherwise, understandably close to the original model's dimensions. Combining the concepts of luxury, as developed in the later 1973 model, with the concepts of sporty lithe quickness so much a part of the original concept, the MUSTANG II brought promise of great and immediate success.

Ford cares about your safety

Ford has been a pioneer in safety design in the automotive industry. Our Safety Research Center has developed stronger, safer, more dependable automotive products for you.

You'll find this reflected in each new 1973 Ford Mustang model which includes these FORD MOTOR COMPANY LIFEGUARD DESIGN SAFETY FEATURES, standard: Improved front and rear bumpers • Improved impact-absorbing laminated safety glass windshield • Dual hydraulic brake system with warning light • Glare-reduced instrument panel padding, windshield wiper arms, steering wheel hub, rearview mirror/mirror mounting and windshield pillars • Energy-absorbing steering column and steering wheel • Energy-absorbing armrests and safety-designed door handles • Front and rear lap belts with mini buckles for all seating positions and retractors for front and rear outboard occupants • Shoulder belts for front outboard occupants • Positive reminder warning light and buzzer for front outboard seat belts • Turn indicators with lane-changing signal feature • Inside yield-away rearview mirror • Energy-absorbing instrument panel with padding for center and outboard passengers • Padded sun visors • Locking steering column with warning buzzer • Two-speed windshield wipers • Windshield washers • Double-yoke safety door latches and safety hinges • Steel guard rails in side doors • Hazard warning flasher • Backup lights • Side marker lights • Energy-absorbing front seat back tops with padding • Self-locking front seat backs on two-door vehicles • Safety-designed coat hooks (except convertibles) • Safety-designed radio control knobs and push buttons (on all cars equipped with radios) • Outside rearview mirror, driver's side • Safety rim wheels and load-rated tires • Corrosion-resistant brake lines • Uniform transmission shift quadrant (on all cars equipped with automatic transmission) • Parking lamps coupled with headlamps • Non-reversing odometer • Safety design front end structure • Head restraints or high back seats for front outboard occupants • Safety glove-box latch (on all cars equipped with glove boxes).

Built-in safety is something you have going for you in every Mustang. Take full advantage of this protection as you drive. Obey all traffic laws, think ahead and always buckle up for safety.

Economy of Operation: All 1973 Mustangs call for 36,000 miles, or 3 years (whichever comes first) between major chassis lubrications, 4,000 miles, or 4 months, between oil changes. Oil filter change initially at 4,000 miles or 4 months, and at 8,000-mile or 8-month intervals thereafter. Other economy features include: self-adjusting brakes, 2-year engine coolant-antifreeze, long-life Motorcraft Sta-Ful battery; corrosion-resistant aluminized muffler, zinc-coated underbody parts, use of regular gas, and more.

	1965	1973		Increase
Wheelbase	108.0"	109.0"	+	1.0"
Overall Length	181.6"	193.8"	+	12.2"
Width	68.2"	74.1"	+	5.9"
Height	51.1"	50.7"	-	0.4"
Track				
Front	55.4"	61.5"	+	6.1"
Rear	56.0"	61.0"	+	5.0"
Trunk Space (cu. ft.)	8.5	9.5	+	1 cu. ft.
Fuel Capacity	16 gal.	19.5 gal.	+	3.5
Curb Weight	2562 lb.	3137 lb.	+	575 lbs.

1974 MUSTANG II, revealed August 23, 1973, was entirely new car.

1973 MUSTANG CONVERTIBLE

*In 1973, the Ford Division's last remaining Convertible appear-
ed in the Mustang line. Changing values, the quiet and comfort
of an air-conditioned closed car, higher freeway speeds (at
least until 1975) had doomed the once-popular "ragtop", and
as they were slowly phased out of domestic production, to be
available only as imported models, their passing was hardly
noticed. Now, almost five years after the last of them was
built, photographs of the 1973 Mustang Convertible leave only
a suggestion of its prevailing charisma.*

Mr. David Mull, Irvine, California

The standard hood (right) has an optional dress-up stripe on the Mach 1 (below). An optional non-functional Tutone hood is again available for all models and the same hood with *functional* air scoops is available with the optional 351 2-V engine.

In addition to new "rectangular" headlamps for 1973, new parking lamps, mounted vertically, replace the former Sportslamps in the grill.

The new color-keyed Urethane front bumper is part of an energy-absorbing bumper system.

The standard grill emblem is placed on a rectangular "egg crate" grill. Mach 1 (and optional on other models) has a new expanded-octagon grill and omits the "corral" (photo above).

Tinted windshield, standard on the Convertible, is formed from a new improved impact-absorbing laminated safety glass.

The Mustang script appears on front fenders of all models including the Mach 1.

Wheel lip and rocker panel moldings are standard on all models except the Mach 1.

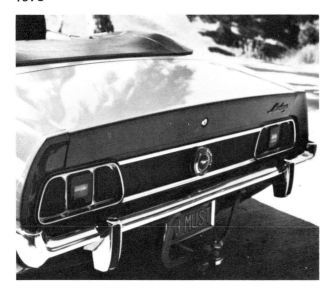

Lower back panel treatment differs; on the Convertible, Hardtop, and SportsRoof, a grained black applique with bright metal moldings is used. A more elaborate honeycomb applique is used on the Grande and the Mach 1 (right). The trailer hitch is an accessory.

The Mach 1 name, reduced in height from the 1972 style (page 289), is applied over the right rear lamp.

Tail lights have a new chromed bezel replacing the earlier style (page 283).

The rear bumper guards are an Option, and are additionally available as a part of the Deluxe Bumper Group which features them together with a rub strip on the bumper itself. Guards are not available for the front bumper.

Convertible and Grande models have deluxe molded door panels with integral arm rests and wood-toned inserts (also available as an Option in the Mach 1).

The window riser handles have a distinctive knob.

The "Safety Standards Certification Label" is again affixed to the left door.

For safety, the inside door latch handle is recessed into the molded door panel.

The standard two-spoke wheel can be optionally replaced with a leather-wrapped wheel, a Tilt Steering Wheel, or by the three-spoke Rim-Blow Deluxe Steering Wheel.

The Convertible standard interior includes deluxe knitted vinyl trim with seatback inserts. A power-operated 4-ply top is standard as is the color-keyed boot.

SelectShift Cruise-O-Matic continues to be Optional, but the mini-console continues as a standard item.

Mustang (or Grande) emblem appears on instrument panel center.

In addition to earlier conventional options, new choices for 1973 include a 3/4 Vinyl Roof for the SportsRoof and Mach 1, new forged aluminum wheels, and a new Protection Group which now includes in addition to side stripe and bumper inserts, a new spare tire lock and door edge guards.

Instrument faces are unchanged.

Again, in addition to the optional AM radio, and AM/FM Stereo or an AM/Stereosonic tape player is offered.

1973

The final Mustang Convertible, the last soft-top to be built by any Ford Division, is Serial Number 3F03Q259417. Built on June 25, 1973, this historically significant car had not yet been titled in 1978, and with only a very few miles on it remains in the possession of Mr. Ron Stoltz, a former Ford Dealer in Pennsylvania.

Grown into maturity, the 1973 model was one end of a line that had been commenced with the light, fast, sporty car of 1964. Almost ten years had passed, and ever-increasing additions had changed the Mustang from what it started out to be. Thus in 1974 the line was to be broken, and an entirely new small and exciting version would appear. Not only was the Convertible gone, so indeed was the car that Mustang had become.

The 1974 Mustang's gait was slowed. No longer at a gallop, it seems to move slower, and smoother, now in a canter.

Gas Caps

Almost every year a new cap was introduced, and this provides a ready reference for Mustang-watchers. Although there has been some overlap, the designs do lend themselves to an annual model designation.

1964½-1965-1965 GT 350

Initially the cap was unsecured (above), but as an early running change, a security wire was introduced (right) and the cap bolted to the car.

1966

1966 GT Models

1966 GT 350

From the start Mustang had a center-fill fuel tank, a feature that permits filling easily from either side of the car.

In addition to the standard 1967 screw-on cap (above) a new pop-open Optional cap appeared (right, and below).

In addition to 1966 style screw-on GT cap (facing page), the 1967 GT and GTA had optional pop-open cap (also used on 1968 GT).

1967 GT 500 gas cap (GT 350 similar)

1968

1968 GT/CS and pop-open Option.

1968 GT 500

1968 GT 500KR

GAS CAPS

1969

1969 GT Models

1969/70 GT 350/500 have conventional cap over fuel filler tube concealed by hinged rear license plate.

1971 Mach 1 has unique stainless steel cap.

1970

Starting with the 1971 models, the security wire was omitted and the cap no longer connected to the car.

1971-73

Wheels
and
Wheelcovers

WHEELCOVERS

Initially offered only on 13" Falcon wheels, tire sizes were 6.50 x 13 standard and 7.00 x 13 with V-8 engines. By September, all V-8's were assembled with 14" Fairlane wheels and standard 6.95 x 14 tires. Black side wall tires are standard; whitewalls are always an extra-cost Option.

Through 1970, wheels used with the SIX have only four bolt holes (above) and those used with V-8's have five. After that, all Mustang wheels have five bolt holes.

Two optional covers for 1964½-65 are the simulated 14" wire wheelcover with spinner (above), and a plain-centered wire cover in both 13" and 14" (right).

The standard black-centered 1965 wheelcover is available in both 13" and 14" versions, and is made in both chromed and rustless steel; either is correct.

An optional cover, the 1965 spinner type is also available in both 13" and 14" in chrome and in rustless steel. A three-segment red, white, and blue ring surrounds the black center.

In 1965, an optional 15" cast aluminum wheel was available for the GT 350. The "Blue Dot" high speed Goodyear tires, standard for the car, were rated at 130 miles per hour.

These 14" Styled Steel Wheels became an Option in 1965 (next page). Optional 6.95 x 14 Dual Red Band tires were standard with all High Performance engine installations.

The attractive 14" Styled Steel Wheel was offered for 1965 (preceeding page) in a "one-piece" construction. Continuing into 1966, its design was then simplified and became a chromed center with an outer chromed ring (above).

Optional Mustang Styled Steel wheel has solid bolt hole web.

The wheel center is dressed with a 2½" Mustang cap.

The 1965-66 hub cap (left) is replaced with a more elaborate unit for 1967.

A Cougar wheel resembles the Mustang wheels but has an opening in the bolt hole web, and its spokes are not "dimpled".

Replacement caps (left) are more securely fastened to wheels with screws in place of earlier spring arrangement.

The Styled Steel Wheel was again an Option for 1967.

The standard full wheelcover has distinctive slots.

There are at least two variants (see centers) although only one part number is listed.

1966

In addition to these choices, the Styled Steel Wheel (previous page) was available in 1966. All standard Mustang wheels and wheelcovers are 14''; tires are 6.95 x 14.

Optional 1966 full wheelcover with center spinner.

1966 simulated wire cover with spinner; also used in early 1967, has blue center (right).

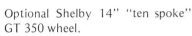

Optional Shelby 14'' "ten spoke" GT 350 wheel.

Optional Shelby five-spoke 15'' GT 350 wheel.

Standard GT 350 and GT 350H 14'' Kelsey Hayes Magnum 500 wheel. Chromed on the Hertz model, it is gray on GT 350.

WHEELCOVERS

1967

Standard 1967 full wheel cover has red center.

Optional full wheelcover, alternately available with plain center, is also used on Falcons and Fairlanes.

Optional Styled Steel 14" wheels for 1967 are also available; see page 308.

Again, all Mustang wheels are 14" and standard tires are black side wall 4 ply 6.95 x 14. Shelby-American offered an optional plain 15" steel wheel (in addition to those shown below) and special "Speedway 350" low profile nylon E70-15 tires.

1967 wire wheel, with red center, is also used through 1969.

Early 1967 GT 350/500 wheelcover.

Optional Styled Aluminum 15" GT 350/500 wheel (above) had chromed steel rim. Another option for those cars, available from Shelby-American, is the ten spoke 15" wheel (right), differing in hub spoke design from 14" version (preceeding page).

Later 1967 and 1968 GT 350/500 wheelcover; similar to Ford part (top photo).

310

1968

Beginning in 1968, this hub cap is standard.

For 1968, tire size remained at 6.95 x 14, but starting in 1969, C78-14 was introduced along with wide oval E70-14 and F70-14 bsw with raised lettering.

1968 optional wheelcover, red center.

Alternate 1968 optional wheelcover, Mustang center.

New optional Styled Steel Wheels for 1968-1969, use separate outer trim ring (right) and either plain or GT hub caps. GT version has thicker cross section but otherwise resembles conventional style.

A blue-center spinner type wheelcover is again listed for 1968 and 1969.

1969

Optional full wheelcover has M-U-S-T-A-N-G center.

15" GT 350/500 wheels are composite (aluminum/steel rim) type with snap-on Cobra hub cap.

Magnum 500 14" wheels, another Mustang option, are standard on BOSS cars.

WHEELCOVERS

1970

Wheels remain at 14". Small hub cap is standard and tires are L78-14 black side walls.

15" chromed Magnum 500 wheel is standard for BOSS cars, an option on others in both 1970 and 1971.

1970 optional full wheel cover has black web and center cap.

Another optional full wheelcover has Mustang center.

1971

1971 optional Sports Wheel Cover has bright web, dark background, but is otherwise similar to 1970 style above.

1971 optional full wheelcover with Mustang center is standard on the Grande, optional on others.

New hub caps and trim rings are another option for 1971.

The standard hub cap with an optional trim ring is again available.

1972 & 1973

The optional Sports Wheelcover (bottom left on facing page) remains unchanged for 1972 and 1973.

Unique wheelcovers are supplied as standard equipment on Grande models.

Optional Magnum 500 wheels are last offered in 1972.

New 1973 Forged Aluminum optional wheel.

The optional 1971 style full wheelcover is offered again in 1972 and 1973.

PRODUCTION FIGURES

Model Year	Body Serial Code	Body Style	Description	Produced	Total
1964½	07	65A	Hardtop	92,705	
	08	76A	Convertible	28,833	121,538
1965	09	63A	Fastback	71,303	
	09	63B	Fastback, Luxury	5,776	
	07	65A	Hardtop	372,123	
	07	65B	Hardtop, Luxury	22,232	
	07	65C	Hardtop, Bench Seat	14,905	
	08	76A	Convertible	65,663	
	08	76B	Convertible, Luxury	5,338	
	08	76C	Convertible, Bench Seat	2,111	559,451
1966	09	63A	Fastback	27,809	
	09	63B	Fastback, Luxury	7,889	
	07	65A	Hardtop	422,416	
	07	65B	Hardtop, Luxury	55,938	
	07	65C	Hardtop, Bench Seats	21,397	
	08	76A	Convertible	56,409	
	08	76B	Convertible, Luxury	12,520	
	08	76C	Convertible, Bench Seat	3,190	607,568

1967	01	65A	Hardtop	325,853	
	01	65B	Hardtop, Luxury	22,228	
	01	65C	Hardtop, Bench Seat	8,190	
	02	63A	Fastback	53,651	
	02	63B	Fastback, Luxury	17,391	
	03	76A	Convertible	38,751	
	03	76B	Convertible, Luxury	4,848	
	03	76C	Convertible, Bench Seat	1,209	472,121
1968	02	63A	Fastback	33,585	
	02	63B	Fastback, Deluxe	7,661	
	02	63C	Fastback, Bench Seat	1,079	
	02	63D	Fastback, Deluxe Bench	256	
	01	65A	Hardtop	233,472	
	01	65B	Hardtop, Deluxe	9,009	
	01	65C	Hardtop, Bench Seat	6,113	
	01	65D	Hardtop, Deluxe, Bench	853	
	03	76A	Convertible	3,339	317,404
1969	02	63A	SportsRoof	56,022	
	02	63B	SportsRoof, Deluxe	5,958	
	02	63C	Mach 1	72,458	
	01	65A	Hardtop	118,613	
	01	65B	Hardtop, Deluxe	5,210	
	01	65C	Hardtop, Bench Seat	4,131	
	01	65D	Hardtop, Deluxe, Bench	504	
	01	65E	Grande	22,182	
	03	76A	Convertible	22,037	
	03	76B	Convertible, Deluxe	3,339	299,824
1970	02	63A	SportsRoof	39,470	
	02	63B	SportsRoof, Luxury	6,464	
	05	63C	Mach 1	40,970	
	01	65A	Hardtop	77,161	
	01	65B	Hardtop, Luxury	5,408	
	04	65E	Grande	13,581	
	03	76A	Convertible	6,199	
	03	76B	Convertible, Luxury	1,474	190,727
1971	01	65D	Hardtop	65,696	
	04	65F	Grande	17,406	
	02	63D	SportsRoof	23,956	
	05	63R	Mach 1	36,499	
	03	76D	Convertible	6,121	149,678
1972	01	65D	Hardtop	57,350	
	04	65F	Grande	18,045	
	02	65D	SportsRoof	15,622	
	05	63R	Mach 1	27,675	
	03	76D	Convertible	6,401	125,093
1973	01	65D	Hardtop	51,480	
	04	65F	Grande	25,274	
	02	63D	SportsRoof	10,820	
	05	63R	Mach 1	35,440	
	03	76D	Convertible	11,853	134,867
			Total 1964-1973 units		2,978,271

The preceeding figures include the following Shelby-American cars:

1965	GT 350	Street Models	550	
		Race Models	12	562
1966	GT 350	Street	1,433	
		Race	3	
		Convertibles	6	
		Hertz	936	2,378
1967	GT 350		1,175	
	GT 500		2,050	3,225
1968	GT 350	Fastback	1,253	
		Convertible	404	
	GT 500	Fastback	1,140	
		Convertible	402	
	GT 500KR	Fastback	933	
		Convertible	318	4,450
	GT 350	Fastback	1,085	
		Convertible	194	
	GT 500	Fastback	1,536	
		Convertible	335	3,150
		Total Shelby-American GT 350/500		13,765

Figures on these pages are from Ford Motor Company and the Shelby-American Automobile Club.

DECODING YOUR DATA PLATE

Owners will find interesting information appearing on the data plates of their vehicles. Although we limit our attention here to the earlier Mustangs, even the later Certification labels starting in 1970 will be found to contain easily decipherable information on Date of Manufacture, etc. Such items as original color, trim, engine, transmission type, etc., can be obtained from these data plates with the cooperation of your local Ford Dealer.

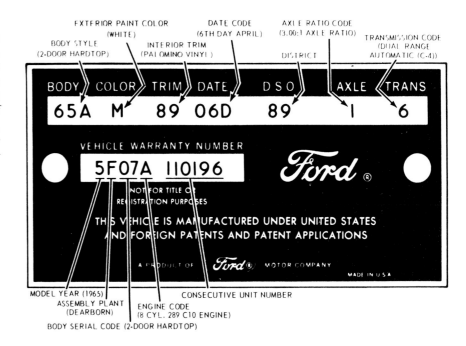

1966/69 data plate differs slightly, but data presented is the same.

Through 1965, a data plate with a black background indicates a unit painted with non-acrylic enamel; gray plate indicates acrylic. Starting in 1966, this was reversed; a black plate thus indicates that *acrylic* enamel was used.

DATE CODES

A number signifying the date precedes the month code letter. A second-year code letter will be used if the model exceeds exceeds 12 months.

Month	Code First Year	Code Second Year
January	A	N
February	B	P
March	C	Q
April	D	R
May	E	S
June	F	T
July	G	U
August	H	V
September	J	W
October	K	X
November	L	Y
December	M	Z

ASSEMBLY PLANT CODES

Code Letter	Assembly Plant	Code Letter	Assembly Plant
A	Atlanta	N	Norfolk
D	Dallas	P	Twin Cities
E	Mahwah	R	San Jose
F	Dearborn	S	Pilot Plant
G	Chicago	T	Metuchen
H	Lorain	U	Louisville
J	Los Angeles	W	Wayne
K	Kansas City	Y	Wixom
L	Michigan Truck	Z	St. Louis

TRANSMISSION CODES

Code	Type
1	3-Speed Manual
5	4-Speed Manual
6	Dual Range Automatic (C-4)

CONSECUTIVE UNIT NUMBER

Each model year, *each* assembly plant begins production with the number 100001, and continues on for each unit built. Since not only Mustangs, but frequently also Falcons and Fairlanes were built on the same assembly lines, the Consecutive Number will include these other models.

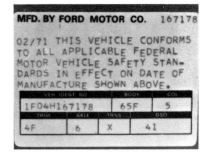

Data appears on Safety Certification Label used starting in 1970.

Exterior Color Code

	1964½	1965	1966	1967
A	Raven Black	Raven Black	Raven Black	Raven Black
B	Pagoda Green	Pagoda Green	—	Frost Turquoise
C	—	Honey Gold	—	—
D	Dynasty Green	Dynasty Green	—	Acapulco Blue
F	Guardsman Blue	—	Light Blue	Arcadian Blue
H	Caspian Blue	Caspian Blue	Light Beige	—
I	—	Champagne Beige	—	Lime Gold
J	Rangoon Red	Rangoon Red	—	—
K	Silversmoke Gray	Silversmoke Gray	Dark Blue Met.	Nightmist Blue
M	Wimbledon White	Wimbledon White	Wimbledon White	Wimbledon White
O	—	Tropical Turquoise	—	—
P	Prarie Bronze	Prarie Bronze	Med. Palomino Met.	—
Q	—	—	—	Brittany Blue
R	—	Ivy Green	Dark Green Met.	—
S	Cascade Green	—	—	—
T	—	—	Candyapple Red	Candyapple Red
U	—	—	Med. Turquoise Met.	—
V	Sunlight Yellow	Sunlight Yellow	Emberglo Metallic	Burnt Amber
W	—	—	—	Clearwater Aqua
X	Vintage Burgundy	Vintage Burgundy	Maroon Met.	Vintage Burgundy
Y	Skylight Blue	Silver Blue	Light Blue Met.	Dark Moss Green
Z	Chantilly Beige	—	Med. Sage Met.	Sauterne Gold
3	Poppy Red	Poppy Red	—	—
4	—	—	Med. Silver Met.	—
5	—	—	Signal Flare Red	—
6	—	—	—	Pebble Beige
8	—	—	Springtime Yellow	Springtime Yellow

BODY STYLE and BODY SERIAL CODE
see page 314

ENGINE CODE
see next page

DISTRICT CODES (DSO)

Units built on a Domestic Special Order, Foreign Special Order, or other special orders will have the complete order number in this space. Also to appear in this space is the two-digit code number of the District which ordered the unit. If the unit is a regular production unit, only the District code number will appear.

Code	District	Code	District
11	Boston	45	Davenport
12	Buffalo	51	Denver
13	New York	52	Des Moines
14	Pittsburgh	53	Kansas City
15	Newark	54	Omaha
21	Atlanta	55	St. Louis
22	Charlotte	61	Dallas
23	Philadelphia	62	Houston
24	Jacksonville	63	Memphis
25	Richmond	64	New Orleans
26	Washington	65	Oklahoma City
31	Cincinnati	71	Los Angeles
32	Cleveland	72	San Jose
33	Detroit	73	Salt Lake City
34	Indianapolis	74	Seattle
35	Lansing	81	Ford of Canada
36	Louisville	83	Government
41	Chicago	84	Home Office Reserve
42	Fargo	85	American Red Cross
43	Rockford	89	Transportation Services
44	Twin Cities	90-99	Export

REAR AXLE RATIO CODES

A number designates a conventional axle, while a letter designates an Equa-Lock differential.

Code	Ratio	Code	Ratio
1	3.00:1	A	3.00:1
3	3.20:1	C	3.20:1
4	3.25:1	D	3.25:1
5	3.50:1	E	3.50:1
6	2.80:1	F	2.80:1
7	3.80:1	G	3.80:1
8	3.89:1	H	3.89:1
9	4.11:1	I	4.11:1

Shelby-American used this data plate under the hood, but removed the Ford data plate on the door thus deleting historical information.

317

Model	1965	1966	1967	1968	1969	1970	1971	1972	1973
6 cylinder									
170 cu. in.	U								
200 cu. in.	T	T	T	T	T	T			
250 cu. in.					L	L	L	L	L
V8									
260	F								
289 2V	C	C	C	C					
289 4V (1964½ only)	D								
289 4V	A	A	A						
289 High-Performance	K	K	K						
302 2V					F	F	F	F	F
302 4V				J					
302 4V Boss					G	G			
351 2V (1)					H	H	H	H	
351 4V (2)					M	M	M	M	M
351 4V Boss (2)							R		
351 4V CJ or GT (2)							Q		
351 4V HO (2)								R	Q
390 2V				Y					
390 4V			S	S	S				
427 4V				W					
428 4V				P					
428 4V CJ					Q	Q			
428 4V JCJ					R	R			
429 4V Boss					Z	Z			
429 4V SCJ							J		

(1) Cleveland or Windsor
(2) Cleveland only

The Mustang used three different six-cylinder engines through 1973, but a much larger number of optional V-8's.

The 260 (used only in 1964½ models), the 289 (last of which was used in 1968), and the 302, which continued through 1973, are all reliable engines with conventional stud-mounted rocker arms and wedge-shaped combustion chambers.

The 351 Windsor engine is a longer-stroke, higher-block version of the 302, so-named for the location of the Foundry in which the block was cast. Introduced in 1969, this 351 was almost immediately joined by another, the Cleveland 351, similar in size, but a more sturdy engine having larger valves, larger main bearings, and a semi-hemispherical combustion chamber. It is furnished with both 2V and 4V carburetion, but the Windsor, with its smaller crankshaft, is limited to 1 2V.

Large-block 390 V-8 engines were offered from 1967 through 1969, and two other large blocks, the 427 and 428 Cobra Jet appeared in 1968. The Boss 302, which appeared in 1969, was essentially a 302 engine equipped with 351 Cleveland heads, and its successor, the Boss 351, was a high-performance version of the 351 Cleveland.

The Boss 429 engine, used in 1968 and 1969, is unique in that it has very large canted valves and a "Crescent" or hemispherical combustion chamber. It also features aluminum heads, uses no head gaskets (O-rings and seals replace it), but it requires special maintenance and repair procedures. It was followed, in 1971, by the 429 Super Cobra Jet, which had special rods, forged pistons, big-valve heads, and an electronic speed limiter set at 6000 RPM.

Last of the offerings was the 351 HO (for High Output), a mid-1972 introduction which was fundamentally the earlier Boss 351 engine now detuned and with reduced compression ratio and full emission controls.

	Displacement	Carburetor	Horsepower	Bore x Stroke	Compression
1965	6-170 CID	IV	105 HP	3.500 x 2.940	9.1/1
	6-200	IV	120	3.680 x 3.126	9.2/1
	8-260	2V	164	3.800 x 2.870	8.8/1
	8-289	2V	200	4.000 x 2.870	9.3/1
	8-289 (1964½ only)	4V	210	4.000 x 2.870	9.0/1
	8-289	4V	225	4.000 x 2.870	10.0/1
	8-289 HP	4V	271	4.000 x 2.870	10.5/1
	8-289 (GT 350)	4V	306	4.000 x 2.870	10.5/1
1966	6-200	1V	120	3.680 x 3.126	9.2/1
	8-289	2V	200	4.000 x 2.870	9.3/1
	8-289	4V	225	4.000 x 2.870	9.8/1
	8-289 HP	4V	271	4.000 x 2.870	10.0/1
	8-289 (GT 350)	4V	306	4.000 x 2.870	10.0/1
1967	6-200	1V	120	3.680 x 3.130	9.2/1
	8-289	2V	200	4.000 x 2.870	9.3/1
	8-289	4V	225	4.000 x 2.870	9.8/1
	8-289 HP	4V	271	4.000 x 2.870	10.0/1
	8-289 GT 350	4V	306	4.000 x 2.870	10.5/1
	8-390	4V	320	4.050 x 3.784	10.5/1
	8-428 GT 500	4V	355	4.130 x 3.984	10.5/1
1968	6-200	1V	115	3.680 x 3.130	8.8/1
	8-289	2V	195	4.000 x 2.870	8.7/1
	8-302	4V	230	4.000 x 3.000	10.0/1
	8-390	2V	265	4.050 x 3.784	9.5/1
	8-390 GT	4V	325	4.050 x 3.784	10.5/1
	8-302 GT 350	4V	250	4.000 x 3.000	10.5/1
	8-428 GT 500	4V	360	4.130 x 3.984	11.6/1
	8-427	4V	390	4.236 x 3.781	10.9/1
	8-428 CJ	4V	335	4.130 x 3.984	10.6/1
1969	6-200	1V	120	3.680 x 3.130	8.1/1
	6-250	1V	155	3.682 x 3.910	9.0/1
	8-302	2V	210	4.000 x 3.000	9.5/1
	8-302 BOSS	4V	290	4.000 x 3.000	10.5/1
	8-351	2V	250	4.000 x 3.500	9.5/1
	8-351C	4V	290	4.000 x 3.500	10.7/1
	8-390	4V	320	4.050 x 3.784	10.5/1
	8-428 CJ	4V	335	4.130 x 3.984	10.6/1
	8-429 BOSS	4V	375	4.360 x 3.590	10.5/1
	8-351 GT 350	4V	290	4.000 x 3.500	10.7/1
	8-302 GT 350	4V	220	4.000 x 3.000	9.0/1
	8-428 GT 500	4V	335	4.130 x 3.984	10.6/1
1970	6-200	1V	120	3.680 x 3.130	8.7/1
	6-250	1V	155	3.682 x 3.910	9.0/1
	8-302	2V	210	4.000 x 3.000	9.5/1
	8-302 BOSS	4V	290	4.000 x 3.000	10.5/1
	8-351	2V	250	4.000 x 3.500	9.5/1
	8-351C	4V	300	4.000 x 3.500	11.4/1
	8-428 CJ	4V	335	4.130 x 3.984	10.6/1
	8-429 BOSS	4V	375	4.362 x 3.590	10.5/1
1971	6-250	1V	145	3.682 x 3,910	9.0/1
	8-302	2V	210	4.000 x 3.000	9.0/1
	8-351	2V	240	4.000 x 3.500	9.5/1
	8-351 BOSS	4V	330	4.000 x 3.500	11.0/1
	8-351 CJ	4V	280	4.000 x 3.500	9.0/1
	8-351C	4V	285	4.000 x 3.500	10.7/1
	8-429 SCJ	4V	375	4.362 x 3.490	11.3/1
1972*	6-250	1V	99	3.680 x 3.910	8.0/1
	8-302	2V	141	4.000 x 3.000	8.5/1
	8-351	2V	164	4.000 x 3.500	8.6/1
	8-351 HO	4V	266	4.000 x 3.500	8.6/1
1973	6-250	1V	99	3.680 x 3.910	8.0/1
	8-302	2V	141	4.000 x 3.000	8.5/1
	8-351	2V	164	4.000 x 3.500	8.6/1
	8-351 CJ	4V	248	4.000 x 3.500	8.0/1

*Commencing in 1972, Horsepower is the SAE net, measured at the rear of the transmission, and with all accessories installed and operating.

Abbreviations: CID: Cubic Inch Displacement HP: horsepower; CJ: Cobra Jet; SCJ: Super Cobra Jet; HO: High Output; C: Cleveland.

	1965	1966	1967	1968	1969	1970	1971	1972
Hardtop	73.3%	82.6%	74.9%	79.2%	43.0%	43.7%	44.7%	46.5%
Fastback	13.8	11.5	14.8	12.9	21.0	20.4	14.7	12.2
Convertible	12.9	5.7	9.3	7.9	4.6	3.9	3.9	5.1
Grande'					7.5	7.0	11.3	14.2
Mach 1					23.9	21.4	14.7	22.0
Boss 302						3.6		
Boss 351							1.1	

RATES FOR TYPICAL OPTIONS
(expressed as a percentage of total production)

	1965	1966	1967	1968	1969	1970	1971	1972
Air Conditioner	9.1	9.5						
Radio	79.6	84.6						
Auto. Trans.	53.6	62.9						
GT Equip. Group	2.7	4.2	5.1	5.5	1.8			
Vinyl Roof	4.9	11.5	15.0	18.5	16.7	16.9	12.9	17.3
Louvered Hood				63.7				
Power Top (Conv.)	8.6	7.5	6.7	6.3	3.4	std	std	std
Disc Brakes	4.4	1.9	11.9	11.6	28.1	30.2	39.7	54.4
Power Steering	23.7	29.0	44.9	52.4	66.2	73.2	85.5	90.0
Convertible glass Backlite			5.4	6.5	3.0			

Figures from Ford Motor Company records.

Readers seeking additional information on the topic might care to contact:

Shelby-American Automobile Club
415 Dorchester Avenue
Reading, Pennsylvania 19609

Publishes *The MARQUE,* a highly professional bi-monthly magazine featuring technical material, classified advertisements, and news of Regional Activities. Holds Annual Convention and Regional Invitationals. Interest directed to Shelby American products including Cobra, Shelby, Tiger, and Ford GT.

The Mustang Club of America, Inc.
Post Office Box 447
Lithonia, Georgia 30058

Published MUSTANG TIMES, a monthly Newsletter featuring technical information, Regional Group news, and classified advertising pertaining to Mustangs 1964½-1969. Holds regional activities and an Annual National Meet.